INVENTORY 98

Racewalking for Fun and Fitness

John Gray

Prentice-Hall, Inc.
Englewood Cliffs, NJ

Prentice-Hall International, Inc., *London*
Prentice-Hall of Australia, Pty. Ltd., *Sydney*
Prentice-Hall Canada Inc., *Toronto*
Prentice-Hall of India Private Ltd., *New Delhi*
Prentice-Hall of Japan, Inc., *Tokyo*
Prentice-Hall of Southeast Asia Pte. Ltd., *Singapore*
Whitehall Books, Ltd., *Wellington, New Zealand*
Editora Prentice-Hall do Brasil, Ltda., *Rio de Janeiro*
Prentice-Hall Hispanoamericana, S.A., *Mexico*

Gray, John
Racewalking for fun and fitness.

Bibliography: p.
Includes index.
1. Walking (Sports)   2. Physical fitness.
I. Title.
GV1071.G7   1985   796.5'1   84-24923

ISBN 0-13-750274-5

ISBN 0-13-750266-4 (PBK)

Foreword

I have known John Gray since I took up distance racing in 1965. We've been good friends and close competitors since then. My first running race that year was the Cathedral ten-mile run in Boston, and my second was the Boston Marathon. I started walking, also in 1965, with a wild half-mile walk indoors at the Fargo Building, and that summer I walked at Taunton in a race that is still held annually. John was in all four of those races as well as in hundreds of others since then.

I can honestly say that I know his attitude toward sports and that I approve of it. His experience is well documented. He has kept records over the years since he started in 1947, and his 36-year total is now well over 60,000 miles.

Like me, he has competed every year in both walking and running races. Also like me, he is convinced of the superiority of walking as an exercise from which almost everyone can benefit.

This book is for the normal person who wants to find the most enjoyable sport possible. Some champions may not agree with all that's written in these pages because there is not enough sacrifice involved. The book's goal, however, is not to make champions but to tell you how to enjoy your exercise and how to benefit from walking for both fun and fitness.

I'm convinced that you'll enjoy John's easygoing ways and that your life will never be quite the same again after reading these pages.

You'll be glad about the change.

Dr. George Lattarulo

Introduction

This book is a family affair. Although only two of the members are racewalking competitors, all of us—my wife, our two daughters, our son-in-law, and myself—are real walkers. In competition, two of us have proved to be fairly good, although hardly world class. The others walk simply because it is man's finest, most enjoyable exercise.

I have been walking competitively since 1950 and have had a few wins over the years, but because age-group competition is, for me, the greatest invention since beer, my best days may well lie ahead of me. At least I won my first national championship, the two-mile indoor walk for men 55 to 59 years old, in the winter of 1982. My older daughter, Linda, who is not the athletic type, took second place in her submaster category, ages 30 to 34, in the same meet.

My other daughter, Kate, is quite an athlete, one of the better tennis players and runners on Cape Cod, and a leading woman walker in New England at distances from twenty kilometers on up.

The competitive angle is of little importance, however, compared to the other benefits of walking. My wife, Mary, hasn't been in a race since I more or less forced her to try it almost twenty years ago; nevertheless, she still rates walking as her favorite year-round exercise. She and Linda hate running (or even listening to people talk about running), but each is as likely as Kate or I to suggest a walk.

What we all gain is a list of benefits that make walking sound like the old patent medicines that were touted as panaceas for everything from hiccoughs to cancer. Once you have given my ideas a try, I won't have to worry about selling you on walking. You'll become an ace salesperson yourself.

This book is written for the ordinary athletes, the ones looking for an enjoyable way to keep themselves trim. It's not going to be much help to the dedicated, championship-seeking walkers because they are too intense to accept my various recommendations to relax and have fun.

The dietary suggestions I make are meant to be broken. The training schedules can be interrupted without any great feelings of guilt. The exercises can be skipped entirely for those of you who, like me, are exercise haters.

In brief, this book is an attempt to show you that walking fast—racewalking—can be fun, can be a nice little part of your life, and can make you feel better, look better, and, perhaps, be a better person.

If you are looking for a guru, however, or for a pseudoreligious experience—the equivalent of the so-called runner's high—I'm afraid you're going to have to look elsewhere. I have been walking and running for over a third of a century, doing both at a reasonably high level (New England championships in walking, top thirty finishes several times in the Boston Marathon in running), and yet I've never known anything in walking or running that equals sex, for one thing, or even the pleasures of a great meal to name another talent of my wife's.

But, you know, if you approach racewalking from my point of view, at least the chances are you will never be disappointed. The sport definitely will deliver all the modest pleasures and benefits that I set forth in these pages. Then, if you happen to be one of the rare ones who actually reach a higher spiritual plane through all your exercise, that will simply be a nice bonus.

And even at my common-sense level, walking does do an amazing number of good things for you. Here's a list of just a few of them:

You will lose weight—that is, you will unless you are presently too thin, in which case you will probably gain weight.

You will feel better about yourself because you will be able to do something well that most people cannot do.

You will have better health. Around four hundred years before Christ, Hippocrates said something like, "Walking is man's best medicine," and that is still true today. Walking gives you all the health benefits of running with hardly any of the attendant injury problems that haunt runners.

You will sleep better. There may be some walkers who do not sleep well, but I haven't heard of them. Walking tires out the entire body and readies you for a fine night's sleep.

You will have a better sex life. Studies have been made on this subject (although I'm not sure just how they were done), and the results are always in favor of both male and female athletes.

You will own bragging rights that will shut up, at least temporarily, the more repulsive talkers among your running friends.

You will meet some interesting new friends. Because walkers are still a comparatively rare breed, walkers tend to be a bit different and hence a bit more interesting than most of the rest of humanity.

You will be an athlete with all the good connotations that that label holds for any individual in America in the 1980s.

You will have a safety valve psychologically for days when things are going wrong. I never took a workout when I was feeling depressed without returning from that workout feeling that the world was a little more in perspective than when I started out. Fast walking is an almost guaranteed cure for the blues.

If any or all of these advantages appeal to you, there is a good chance that racewalking is the activity for you. Since it costs practically nothing in equipment (the price of a good tennis racket could finance your walking for years), why not give the sport a chance?

You think you have been walking all your life, but until you try fast walking, you really haven't walked. Try it. You can't lose a thing—except a few inches around your middle.

Contents

1

Why Walk?

Before you can answer the question as to why you, of all people, should take up fast walking, you have to know what kind of walking it is.

Well, it is racewalking, or heel-and-toe walking as they used to call it in the old days, a name that tells you one key part of the definition of walking: You must always have one foot on the ground—that is, one toe must not leave the ground until the other heel touches down.

Besides that, the body must be erect and each leg must straighten out at some point on each stride. Normal street walking, of course, satisfies that definition (although a low-to-the-earth, Groucho Marx type of walk does not; Groucho never straightened out his legs). Normal walking, however, is limited in its effectiveness, and over the years, men and women have devised the racewalking form that is the key to all fast walking.

You are sure to have seen this style. It is a favorite with funny television commercials or moments of comedy in films. The laughs all come from the widely swaying rear ends of the walkers, but the hip motion is worth the ridicule it brings because it is the secret of why fast walking is almost totally injury free.

You see, the hips are not just moving around in a sexually provocative manner; they are being dropped forward and swung to the side simultaneously in such a way that the upper body never

1

rises or falls. All of this will be explained in detail in a later chapter. For now, it is enough for you to know that the body does not slam down on the foot at each stride as in running but instead glides smoothly along.

The result is twofold: First, your body doesn't have to take all those repeated shocks; second, the smoothness of the technique means that you can walk fast much further than you can run, and do so far more pleasantly. Of course, running gets you places faster. There is no denying that, although if you learn to walk and then enter a running race of five miles or more you will almost surely have the great pleasure of beating a few runners. My friend Bob Falciola, a good but not great walker, walked the New York City Marathon and finished in about four hours, ahead of over six thousand officially entered runners. Another friend, Barbara Clark, regularly beats five or ten runners in local five-mile races on Cape Cod or in the Boston area.

Who Should Walk?

Obviously, walkers as good as Bob or Barbara should be walking, but why should ordinary people do so? Well, not everyone should take up walking, but with few exceptions the people who should walk fall into several divisions. First, there are the runners who suffer various injuries because of the pounding their legs take at each stride. Obviously, they would be better off walking for twelve months of the year instead of running for one month and resting with an injury the next.

A second group of people who should try walking are those like my daughter Linda and my wife. They hate running. Fast walking appeals to them because for some magic reason (I'll get to that later) the things that make them hate running are pleasantly absent in walking.

My third group of walk prospects is made up of those who are looking for an exercise that builds up the whole body without the dreariness that is inherent in most exercise classes (no matter how skillfully Richard Simmons and others may try to hide that dreariness). Walking does almost the same thing as running does for the legs, but it also gives the arms, shoulders, waist, and hips an equally rugged workout. I tend to feel the workout most in my arms and shoulders on the day after a race. I can play several sets of tennis in an afternoon with less exercise than a twenty-kilometer walk gives my arms.

The fourth group (oh, there are so many people who are going to find walking to their liking) consists of those who are looking for a way to lose weight pleasantly. Once you even out your weight by sensible diet (I don't mean harsh dieting, just eating moderately), you will have a gradual weight loss if you stick to that same amount of food and commence walking fast as little as two miles three times a week.

The weight loss will be very slow if you only are going out three times a week for a half hour, but it will be definite. Although weight-reduction charts tell you that you have to walk seventy-two hours to lose a pound, the kind of walking they are talking about is your stroll-to-the-store walk, and that stroll bears about the same relation to fast walking that the dog paddle bears to the Olympic crawl. I have never yet met a man or woman who took up racewalking and stayed with it for over a month without dropping unwanted weight. Conversely, if you are skinny and trying to add weight, walking will do that too because the muscles in your arms and legs will develop, as will the lungs and chest. (See Chapter 10, *How Can You Gain Extra Upper Body Strength?*) I told you that walking was going to sound like the old-time quack remedies. The difference is that walking is for real.

The fifth group to take up walking should be the very competitive runners who simply can't run well enough to meet their own goals. They end up far behind where they feel they should be, and they are unhappy. They can't work any harder, so what should they do? Find another sport as close to running as possible but calling for different body skills for success. It's a simple mathematical fact that half of all runners would do worse in a walk, and the other half would do better. Bill Rodgers, Joan Benoit, and the rest of the runners at the top would be good walkers, but they would not be world champions. They would be foolish to switch sports.

Many of the rest of the runners would do better. I belong to this group. As a runner, I once finished eighth in the Yonkers Marathon when it was a national championship. In another year, I was twenty-first at Boston (a long time ago when the field was slightly over 200). But I never won a championship, not even a New England title. By contrast, I have several New England walking titles in my distant past plus the already mentioned national in my age group. And after I hit the age of sixty in 1984, I then had a chance at lots of championships.

A better example than myself is Tom Knatt of Concord. Tom was a serious runner who finally realized that he was never going to win the Boston Marathon or even break two and a half hours. He was very good but he lacked the physical attributes to become a champion. So he switched to walking years ago and by now has won numerous New England titles, has earned himself overseas trips as a race walker, and is almost totally involved in the sport.

There is a sixth group of prospective walkers made up of people who like to be leaders, not followers. Although walking is increasing by leaps and bounds (a bad cliché to use because leaping and bounding will get a racewalker disqualified), it started from such a small number of walkers just a few years ago that you may well be the first walker in your neighborhood. If the pioneer spirit is strong in you, that could be enough to get you started as a walker.

A final group is perhaps the largest of all and includes over half the women in the country. These are the women with normal-sized or large breasts. Have you ever looked at the women in a running race? Many of them are beautiful, but very few sport the chest of which *Playboy* stars are made. This is not because large-breasted women are inherently unathletic, but because the bouncing involved in distance running is anything but enjoyable. Obviously, if the torso does not go up and down each stride, the bouncing will be practically eliminated.

Who Should Not Walk?

As you can see from the seven divisions of hot prospects for racewalking, it is a sport that holds something for just about everyone except two groups of people. One of these groups is made up of exercise haters, the type of people who go around spouting the old joke that "I get my exercise as a pallbearer for all my friends who love exercise." Such people are not going to enjoy fast walking because it most definitely is hard exercise (although it is only as hard as you want it to be).

The second group of people who should not bother to try walking is made up of those great runners—the Joan Benoits, the Rod Dixons, the Alberto Salazars—who are making a fabulous living from running, or who are the best local runners who are getting a regular ego boost from the local weekly's sports column.

If running has been wonderful to you, if you have earned fame and glory, and if you have never had a running injury, don't switch. You are one of the lucky ones. You have found your niche and should enjoy it.

However, most runners are not that well off, and they ought to give walking a try. Some of them won't like it. There are disadvantages to walking compared to other sports, and I'd better deal with them honestly right here in Chapter 1.

Disadvantages of Walking

First of all, there is the ridicule factor. If you head out for home and racewalk past the local elementary school at recess time, some of those kids are going to hoot at you and your rear end. Wherever you go, you are going to find older louts with grammar-school brains, and they will give you the predictable clichés (worse for women than for men, of course).

Somehow you have to harden yourself to this. For me, it simply is a matter of remembering my early days of running. Runners were an oddity in the 1940s and 1950s, and I got plenty of remarks like, "Hey, mister, you forgot your pants"; or, "Are you going swimming?"; or "Hey, sweetie, you've got nice legs."

One day, a man shouted, "Hey, you a boxer?" Inspired, I simply nodded my head and brushed my nose with the back of my thumb, the way boxers always did in the old movies. It worked. No one razzes a boxer. So I went around strange areas taking little jabs at my own nose, and the remarks ended. More to the point, remarks usually end after you have established yourself as a neighborhood regular. I was a school teacher for over thirty years, always running in my free time, but even though teachers are open game for wise remarks, I seldom had a student make fun of my walking.

So the wise remarks are never as bad as you think they are going to be; but still, if you are really sensitive, you may want to emulate my friend Paul Schell. Paul is a wonderful person, but he can't tolerate being made fun of. He never trained in public, even the year he won a national walking championship. Paul would train after dark at a high-school track. If another person showed up to do some jogging, Paul would stop walking and turn to running as being a less ridiculous form of exercise.

A second disadvantage of walking for those who are competitively inclined is the scarcity of races. On Cape Cod alone, over forty running races a year are held. My current edition of *Ohio Racewalker* lists only forty-six walking races in the entire country over a two-month period. That's the bad news. The good news is that these forty-six races are far more than would have been listed even two years ago, and they are widespread, covering New England; New York; Michigan; Washington, D.C.; Virginia; Arkansas; Missouri; Iowa; Colorado; California; and others.

Barbara Clark may have found the solution to the problem of so few races. Barbara is the owner of Le Gourmet, a store that offers fabulous foods and drinks, and she needed an exercise to protect her from the potential ravages of becoming her own best customer.

When she found racewalking, she loved it, but she did not want to travel all over New England to walk in races. Her solution was to enter running races and walk. Every runner she passes represents a triumph for her.

You can always do that. You also will find yourself walking faster in practice than some poor misguided plodding jogger. Besides the feeling of triumph you get when you ease past that jogger, beating a runner is one of the best ways of advertising the fact that he or she is one of the many people who ought to take up walking.

Another difference between running and walking, one that may or may not be a disadvantage for you, is that walking demands that you constantly monitor your style. In running, you pretty much go as fast as you can with nothing more taxing mentally than worrying about burning yourself out too soon. In walking, however, you have to think about all sorts of stylistic subtleties, things that will keep you walking properly even when you start to tire.

For myself, I enjoy the challenge of knowing that I have to do something precisely correctly if I want to succeed. The challenge adds to the fun of the sport rather than detracting from it. And the heaviest of this pressure comes only in a race when a judge may be lurking behind any rock or tree, ready to give you the dreaded first warning. In practice, walking is as carefree as you want to make it. You can go all out if that is what your schedule has planned for you, but you can also ease off to an easy, stylish walk a couple of minutes a mile slower than your best pace. Such walking is pleasurable, and because you are not bobbing up and down, you get a better view of your surroundings, a better chance to enjoy nature than if you were running.

2

How to Start Walking

This is the easiest chapter in the book, a good one for building confidence. We all started our walking career when we were one or two years old. In your current endeavor to get into fast walking, all you have to do is get up and start to walk. You don't need any stretching exercises, any special equipment, or any complicated technical advice. Just leave your seat, get to your feet, and take to the street. As you have been walking these many years and have never yet pulled a hamstring or strained an Achilles tendon, you are not going to have anything to worry about this time in the way of injuries.

The First Workout

As you walk along slowly, you gradually will feel your body loosen as it does with exercise. If you are really young, really supple, you may be totally loose right from the start. But if you are old or have arthritic tendencies as I do, you may look slightly crippled at first. However you feel for the first few strides, after a few minutes you will be moving along easily at your normal pace, one that would

7

move you about two and a half or three miles if you kept at it for an hour. Within a month we will have you moving at nearly twice this speed.

After you know that the various parts of your body are lubricated and ready to go, start to move faster. Don't try for any fancy racewalking techniques. Just walk fast—as though you were late for an appointment but were too well dressed to run. Walk fast enough so you start breathing hard.

This fast walk is going to get you tired. When you feel yourself starting to strain a little, slow down to the stroll you started out with. Move along easily until you are no longer puffing. Then walk fast again for a bit.

The question as to how far you should go at the fast clip and how long the recovery stroll should be cannot be answered precisely. In this area, as in most of racewalking, you are the coach. You must monitor yourself and decide when you are getting tired. In the first outings, it is better to err on the side of too little. While you can't spoil things by taking it too easy, you can ruin things by overdoing it. For example, if you have an undetected heart condition, and on your first walk you drive yourself to the point of a heart attack, you can end your career for a lot more than just racewalking.

Check with Your Doctor

That extreme, highly unlikely example reminds me of something I should make clear right from the start. Although walking is a very inexpensive sport, you should invest $100 or so in yourself before you even take a step. That's about what it will cost you to have your doctor give you a thorough physical examination.

If you are a sensible person, you already will have had a recent examination, but for some reason most Americans who would not think of driving their cars around without a checkup every three months or so will drive their bodies for years without seeing a doctor.

Thus, unless you are switching from running to walking, you are going to be doing more with your body than you have done since you were a kid. To make sure you are ready for this move up the activity scale (and down on the weight scale), you must see your doctor.

So now we have a certified healthy you out on your first training walk. If you are really pudgy, weak, and sedentary, you may find that the distance between one telephone pole and the next is enough fast walking to get you puffing. So you do the old Boy Scout routine of one telephone pole fast, one (or two or three) slow, and so on.

At the other extreme of fitness, an experienced runner may find that he or she can move along at the fast normal walk for five or ten minutes before feeling the strain. Because regular street walking is so inefficient for a fast pace, even a trained marathoner out for his first walk will start to feel tired in ten minutes. You should take note of this because you will then take extra satisfaction a month or two from now when you will be able to walk many times as far without exhaustion because of the greater efficiency of racewalking style.

As you alternate your fast walks and your recovery periods, whether you are going fifty yards or a mile in each interval, you must make an important judgment as to when you are half tired. At this point, you turn around and head back. It is perfectly all right to go in a circle, of course, but I recommend the out-and-back course because one way of telling if you are trying too much too soon is to check the difference in effort between the first half of your workout and the second half. If the two take you approximately equal times, you are doing just about the right amount. If the second half is laborious and lasts significantly longer, you are pushing too hard, too early. The total walking time should be between fifteen minutes (meaning that you have covered about a mile) and an hour. Even if you are used to jogging for two hours, you should limit yourself to an hour's walking. The muscles are being used in a slightly different way, and you don't want to take a chance on crippling yourself.

The Second Workout

The next day or the day after that—the schedule you have decided on will determine how often you work out in a week, but every other day is a good idea for beginners—you will probably notice a stiffness in your legs. This will disappear as you walk along, but the initial period of slow strolling may have to be longer than on your first day. If you really are in distress on the second outing, don't try any fast walking at all. Then the next time you do feel better and do some fast intervals again, please remember that you might have a tendency to drive your body too hard. Take it easy. Remember that at the end of every workout you should feel that you could have done more. The only time you should drive yourself anywhere near to your limits is when you are in an important race.

Assuming that your second workout finds you feeling all right, you should walk at the same pace as you did the first time, only a little farther. That means another telephone pole or another block or another lap—nothing major, just a slight moving up on the distance scale. You are going into walking as a way of life. Later on, I will be telling about men who walked competitively well into their eighties. So there is no rush. (If you think about it, the really soft walker who starts out unable to go more than five telephone poles away from the driveway will be going 370 poles away at the end of a year, simply by adding one a day. Telephone poles vary in their distances apart, but three of them will usually total more than 100 yards, 50 of them at least a mile. So that two times 370 means that you can be up to fourteen miles by the end of a year.)

Developing Technique

When you have gotten your body used to doing intervals for a week or so, you will be ready to add some technique lessons to your workout. I suggest that even runners in superb shape should delay the racewalking style for a week even though their bodies are ready for anything. The reason for this delay is the psychological difficulty of the racewalking style. You are going to move awkwardly at first, and you would feel foolish even if your walking were perfectly smooth. But looking awkward and having your rear end moving wildly (it will feel worse than it looks, but it will look odd enough anyway) can make you feel so uncomfortable that you dread going out. That's bad.

Let me save you time right from the start. You are taking up walking because you are looking for the most enjoyable form of exercise. If you find you hate it—and some people will—don't press on. Give it a fair trial, a month or so, and if you still hate it, quit. Go back to lifting weights, to Richard Simmons, to massage-and-diet programs, or to being just plain soft and fat. If walking or any other exercise is not enjoyable, it's not worth doing.

Anyway, after a week or two you are ready for your first technique workout. It starts like any other workout with a stroll and then the usual fast-walk interval. At the end of this interval, take twenty fast steps, marking where you start and where you finish. Then go back to the starting line and take twenty strides again, only this time reach as far forward as possible on each stride.

To get the maximum length on each stride, you will find that you have to drop the leading hip. This is the start of the racewalking hip girdle, which actually drops the hip about twice as far as it moves it to the side. To give yourself some balance, you will have to move your arms more vigorously than normal. Bend your arms at a 90-degree angle at the elbow.

These two things, the drop and reach with each stride and the vigorous pumping of the arms, straight forward and straight back, will give you added distance. It doesn't take a great mathematician to figure out that if you reach out farther with your foot, you are going to cover more ground with your twenty strides (Figure 1).

As you take these twenty strides with your new form, you should find that you have covered the same distance as your twenty normal strides by the time you reach eighteen strides of the fast-walking style.

Once you are satisfied that you have gained a longer stride by your new form, you can stop measuring and start trying to feel comfortable with the new form. You will probably want to divide your interval training into three parts now: the easy stroll, the normal fast walk, and the new race-walking style.

Your goal is to drop the fast regular walk (which leaves your body going up and down on every stride) and do only form walking, fast or slow. Again, it is impossible to determine in advance when you will reach the point in your training at which you do both the fast and slow stages in race-walking form.

Figure 1

Kate Gray demonstrates a good style for a beginner to study. Note the angle at the elbow; the left arm comes back so high that it is nearly parallel with the shoulders. The right arm has come forward a little too high, and the left leg does not reach out as far forward as it would with a more pronounced hip girdle, but the body is erect. This is a style that a beginner can achieve fairly quickly.

I will tell you about my first coaching experience to show you what I mean. Two friends and I started women's race walking in Lowell and Taunton, Massachusetts, in 1964. Tony Medeiros, a former top-ten finisher in the Boston Marathon, had turned to walking and eventually became a frequent national champion in his age group. He put on one of the two big walks in New England, a Labor Day walk from Lawrence to Lowell, and had a young protégée who was outstanding: Nancy was thirteen years old and a beautiful walker.

Win Benton, who organized the other big New England walk in Taunton, also got some girls interested. I talked my older daughter, Linda, and two of her friends into trying. The first women's walk was a five-mile race before the men's race, and the three girls I coached finished in just the reverse order of what I expected. Marcia, the athlete of the three, never could get the smooth stride and was fighting herself all the way, finishing sixth out of the dozen in the race. Linda walked barefoot, and because her feet were tough and her style was pretty good, she sailed smoothly through the five miles, finishing fourth behind a Taunton girl and Esther Smith, a woman about fifty years old. The winner of the race was Marcia's cousin Ann, the least athletic of the three, one of those thirteen year olds who are already putting much of their lives into being beautiful. She not only had a beautiful face, but she also had flawless form, and she won easily.

I had given them all the same advice, but the technique took effect almost immediately with Ann. It would have taken weeks for Marcia to have reached the level that her cousin achieved in a few days. (None of the three girls took the race too seriously.)

Those early races for women were ahead of their time. We developed one outstanding walker, Nancy, who joined the field in the second year. Unfortunately, Nancy found a boyfriend who hated to see her wiggling her bottom around the streets, and he got her to quit. The whole thing died out, and no one heard of women's walking races in New England again until the 1980s.

I went into that long digression to show you that you should not be discouraged if your feel for the technique of walking develops slowly. I want to help you start out more like Ann than like her athletic cousin.

Summarization of Technique

To summarize what you need in the way of technique to start out, I can tell you to concentrate on two things. First, drop your hip and swing it to the side on each stride. The drop is about two or three times as much as the swing to the side. You will do this hip action fairly naturally if you concentrate on reaching out with your foot just as far as you can on each stride (Figure 2).

Second, get your arms into the act. Keep them at about a ninety-degree angle and pump them vigorously forward and backward on each stride. If you hold a tennis racquet or yardstick in each hand, and move your arms far enough to move the racket or stick out of your line of peripheral vision each time you bring your arms back, you will be on the right track. Also try to move your arms straight forward as though you were punching a bag.

That is enough technique for the beginning stages. If you go into walking only for exercise, not for racing, this may be all the technique you will ever need. The two things I have emphasized will get your whole body into action, as you will be well aware the first day you try it.

Again, don't forget to take it comparatively easy the first time you try your racewalking technique. You may well find that the hip and arm action combine to overwork your middle, and you will start to feel a cramp in your side. If you do, simply slow to a stroll, bend

Figure 2

When you first start to work on the hip girdle, there is no need to aim for an extreme form. Here Kate has a slight hip girdle. It is effective because it is smooth, she keeps her balance, and her feet land in a direct line, one with the other.

slightly forward, leaning into the cramp, and rub the spot gently as you go along.

If you have never had a cramp before, you may feel panicky, but it is really nothing to worry about. I don't fully understand the medical facts behind cramps, but you will find all you need to know in Chapter 15, written by Dr. George Lattarulo, a man who specializes in long-distance walks (100 kilometers and 100 miles). George will tell you more than I personally want to know, but I realize that I am a bit too casual about health and safety and understanding my own body.

Walking with a Partner

There is one final thing the beginning walker needs, and that is advice from more than this book. For example, walking technique is much easier to understand if you can see yourself in action. As I don't expect you to have your own video equipment, I have a different and better suggestion for seeing yourself as others see you: Get a friend to start walking with you.

The loneliness of the long-distance walker was never an ideal; it was a reality only because walkers and runners were both such a scarce commodity. Now there are untold millions of runners, and just the women runners in America now outnumber the total number of men who ran marathons in the first sixty-five years of this century. That is not saying much because the Boston Marathon always had between 200 and 250 starters for those sixty-five years. And that was with no qualifying standards at all. The best runners were always very good, but the medal winners (up to thirty-fifth place) would come in over half an hour behind the winner, and the thirty-fifth man seldom finished in under three hours.

So you don't have to be lonely. Check back over the seven types of people who will probably enjoy fast walking when they learn about it. You may even find that you are married to or dating one of them. Walking fast with a friend is the ultimate in pleasant exercise. You have time and breath for conversation, and the miles slip by more easily than in any other way I have ever discovered.

You should use some discretion in selecting your partner. If your best friend or lover is in fantastic shape and you are a pudgy blob of good intentions, go out with your second best friend. Two mismatched friends will always find one bored and unchallenged, benefiting little from the workout, while the other is frantic, overextended, and in danger of crippling his or her body by making every day's workout into a life-or-death struggle.

You can match strides with partners of somewhat varying abilities, but opposite ends of the fitness scale should settle for a post-workout beer together. The exception is the pair willing to do their workouts on a track. One person's speed lap can be the other's recovery lap, and they can thus match strides for half the workout.

Where to Walk

I hardly recommend tracks as a location, however. You should enjoy your walking. For me here on Cape Cod that means beaches at low tide, country roads, anywhere early in the morning before people are up, and most of all (because it is the only place my three dogs can go safely with me) along the power lines.

If you look around your area, you will find attractive places. Don't always settle for your own neighborhood. It is worth a ten-minute drive to get to a really nice place. Always keep in mind the fact that you are out to enjoy walking, and, believe me, scenery helps.

The local high school track has the undeniable advantage of accurate distance, and as you will see in the chapter on advanced training, I recommend it on a twice-a-month basis to check your progress. However, it is seldom the most beautiful area, and the repetition of scenes is something less than thrilling. You will go past everything twenty times during a five-mile workout.

For A Successful Start

You now can see that getting started as a walker is not terribly complicated. Once you get past the psychological difficulty of going public with an exaggerated swing in your caboose, you have only five things to concentrate on for a successful start:

1. Plan the time to take your walks. Schedule them for at least three days a week, not on a "Maybe I'll feel like it tomorrow" basis. Make three or more definite appointments with yourself.

2. Search for places to walk. Find places that are attractive either because of their natural loveliness or because they are fascinating parts of the city.

3. Convince a friend that walking will be fun for the two of you together.

4. Alternate your walking between easy warmup and recovery periods and fast intervals that get you breathing hard.

5. Work on your technique. Drop the hip and reach out as far as possible on each stride, working your arms vigorously to help with this increased stride.

3

What Should You Wear?

*T**he question of clothing** and shoes is yet another area in which common sense will hold you in good stead. If it's comfortable, it's good. That's really all the advice that anyone needs.

For those who like to benefit from others' errors, I can point out times that I've worn the wrong clothing. For example, in cold weather you must dress to keep warm, but you could do something foolish as I did on one of my earlier long outings along the beach.

I started out easily enough, nice and warm, and all went well. The trouble came when I got very warm and started to perspire heavily. I had been walking with a fifteen-mile-per-hour breeze directly behind me and the sun beating down on me. I was soaked through at the end of an hour when I turned around for the five-mile walk home.

Suddenly, what had been a light breeze seemed to double in speed as I headed directly into it. The sun went behind clouds for the hour's walk home, and the wind seemed terribly cold as it whipped through my wet outfit.

I became colder and colder, went slower and slower, and was thoroughly miserable for the whole trip back, a trip that took me nearly an hour and a half because I actually had gone closer to six than to five miles on the way out, when it was all so easy with the wind behind me. I had made two errors. The clothing was okay for the first half of the workout but not for the second half, and I had done the easy half first and left the tough part for the tired half. What I needed was a windbreaker that I could tie around my waist and have ready for the wind. And I should have walked into the wind for the first half, and saved the breezy, easy part of the day for when I was tired. Actually, you could probably figure out something like that yourself, but maybe I will save a few of you from taking a thoughtless workout when a thinking person's workout would have been equally simple and much less unpleasant.

Clothing

More to the point for ordinary workouts, I can tell you that I prefer cotton next to my skin rather than the various synthetics. Cotton is good stuff, and although you should feel free to experiment, most of you are going to like cotton the best.

Much of your clothing will be chosen for its looks, and here your vanity and your finances will have to battle it out. There are good-looking outfits available for both sexes, and if you want to spend a couple of hundred dollars, you can let the general public know that you are serious about your walking. But you can also go out in an old shirt and pants and get the same physical benefits. You just won't look as flashy.

One thing everyone should investigate is the unisex running shorts that are obviously unisex walking shorts as well. These are one-piece shorts that incorporate an inner panties-like support garment that works well. They are the lightest possible clothing for any day you're serious about your performance, and they come in a great variety of colors. They also come in a great variety of prices, and you will find yourself paying extra for the right to wear a famous runner's initials on your shorts. I always buy the cheapest things that fit. I seem to enjoy my sport more for knowing that it's such a bargain.

Shoes

If I tend to shop parsimoniously for my clothing, I do not aim for cheapness in my shoes. Shoes are vital, and you will get pretty much what you pay for. The bargain shoe may have stripes similar to those on the expensive model, but the shoe itself will be a distant and very poor relation of the best.

Even with good shoes, walking is the least expensive activity you engage in. As it becomes popular, there will undoubtedly be the fastbuck artists who try to sell you a variety of ridiculous things, but I can tell you from long experience that all you need can be purchased at an annual cost of less than $100.

I am extremely easy on shoes myself, and I like to put it this way: I manage to walk for about two and a half cents per mile. I buy one pair of shoes a year, always waiting for a good sale. I use Shoe Goo to extend the life of these shoes—that's three dollars more. My warm-up suit cost $30 about ten years ago, for another annual three-dollar expense. I get two years out of my $10 North Medford Club running suits. And socks cost me the most of all, as I wear out four or five pairs a year at up to three dollars a pair.

Anyway, I walk and run about 2,000 miles a year on that $50 investment, and I submit that that is cheap entertainment—about fifteen cents per hour's exercise. You can't even buy a candy bar or a good cigar for fifteen cents any more, but in walking you can buy a whole new world of fun and exercise. How can you pass up such a bargain?

The question of shoes is the major one in walking. There are lots of great shoes for runners on the market, but the walkers have far less to choose from. I can pass on to you what I have learned from my June 1982 issue of the *Ohio Racewalker* and from my own experience.

The problem with even the best running shoes is that they have the wrong heels and the wrong cushioning for walking. The cushioning is vital for the runner, who risks pounding himself to destruction. It is not needed in walking. The roll heel that most running shoes have is simply "not really desirable for race walking" according to the *Ohio Racewalker* article.

In running, the foot lands almost flat; but in proper walking the heel strikes first while the foot is at a forty-five-degree angle to the ground. If the shoe has a thick mid-sole, the cushioning reduces the amount of flexibility in the forefoot area and gives more protection (and thus weight) than is needed. At the heel, the top edge of the shoe curves inward in most running shoes, digging into the Achilles tendon area. This can cause problems for runners, but it is likely to be more acute for walkers.

Companies have produced special walking shoes over the years, but the problem is that they can be difficult to obtain because there aren't many around. In addition, styles change frequently, so even if you find a good pair, you are left to start your search all over again when that pair wears out.

It would be foolish to name specific models for you to purchase because the styles change faster than books get published. It does make sense, however, to give some general advice. Basically, you have little choice but to walk in a running shoe. Here are eight hints for finding the proper shoe:

Hints for Shoes

1. Look for good brand names. My own favorites—and I have worn all of these—are New Balance, Etonic, Rebek, Tiger, Nike, Adidas, Converse, and Saucony. There are other good brands, and none of them are cheap.

2. Shop around for prices. Discount stores often sell the same shoe at real savings compared to larger chain stores. Never put price first, but if you can go to the New Balance outlet store, for example, you have a tremendous choice, and the prices are all good.

3. Read the latest shoe ratings in magazines, and then choose for yourself among the many good shoes mentioned.

4. Remember that you are buying a running shoe to walk in, and that means that many models simply are not quite right for you. In fact, as running shoes have gotten better and better for running, they have in many cases become less suitable for serious walking. Thus, you must be careful when buying a pair. Among the things to avoid in running shoes are: a too-thick heel (the runner needs protection that a walker does not need); too much sole protection up front, something that reduces the flexibility for the walker; and a heel cup that curves inward and that can dig into the Achilles tendon, causing a problem for walkers, who have that angled heel landing.

5. Search for shoes made specifically for racewalking. There aren't many yet, and they tend to go out of production quickly, but as the numbers of serious walkers increase so too will the numbers of shoes made properly for the walker.

6. Most of all, make sure that the shoe you wear is comfortable for you. Try on many pairs. Walk around the store. Don't rush through the process, and don't buy a shoe just because an ad (or even a friend) tells you how great it is. Only your foot can be the final coach and advisor as to where to put your money.

7. Once you have found a good shoe, there are two ways for you to proceed. One, favored by many top walkers, is to find the best shoe and then buy several pairs so you always wear the best, practice or race, rain or shine. It certainly makes sense to go with the best, but I

have a different method that also has some advantages. Whenever I see a shoe at a bargain price, I try it on. If my foot approves, I buy it. I now wear a dozen different shoes made by five different companies. They are all good. I find that a change of shoes brings a certain comfort. For an extreme example, suppose you have two places on your feet that tend to blister, even with the best of shoes. And suppose that one pair causes you to blister more in one place, the other in another. Obviously by rotating the shoes, you will give your feet a better chance to avoid serious blisters. Another advantage to having several favorite shoes is that when one model goes out of production, you still have four good ones left to choose from, but if you have only one favorite shoe, you can feel abandoned when the shoe no longer exists. You may even then be tempted to wear the shoe after it has worn down too far to be safe.

8. That brings us to the final rule. Protect your shoes with Shoe Goo, Shoe Patch, or some other substance that saves the sole. (Sole Saver is my favorite name among such products.) If a shoe wears down seriously on the heel, almost always on just one side of the heel, then on every stride the shoe is throwing your body slightly out of kilter, and the cumulative effect of such a slight out-of-line stride can be an eventual injury or serious strain on your system.

In brief, the message of this chapter is don't waste money on clothes and don't try to pinch pennies on shoes. Clothes are simply for comfort and for beauty; shoes are for survival.

I can't end this chapter without a final word about the unimportance of clothing. The old-time pedestrians, of whom you will learn in Chapter 19, were unbelievably formal in their attire. They wore quite natty outfits, although nothing like today's chic warmup suits. The old-timers went in for business clothes, complete with neckties, dapper collars, and a whole outfit of Victorian propriety. Such clothes must have slowed down the wearer somewhat, but the fabulous feats of the nineteenth-century walkers still are impressive today, including fifty miles in seven hours and frequent outings of over five hundred miles in six days. There is no doubt as to the authenticity of these records because the inspiration of them all was gambling, and with thousands of dollars at stake you can be sure that no one was permitted to fudge the results in any way.

Thus, today you really can wear anything you want during your training. Just keep this simple advice in mind:

"If it feels good, wear it."

4

How Do You Protect Yourself from Injury?

W_alking is inherently injury-free;_ thus, your chief protection is built into the sport. You are already protected from injury by the naturalness of your activity. Still, the habit of good warmup exercises is an added protection.

Warmup

I myself hate exercises, and I avoid them. I know that my methods are hardly standard. Everyone else seems to agree that warmup exercises are vital to injury-free participation in any sport. My own warmup, as I have told you, is totally casual. When I go out for a workout, whether walking or running, I walk along at a normal slow pace. Then I gradually stretch the muscles by walking very slowly in an exaggerated racewalk style. I suppose that I take close to ten minutes to cover the first half mile. Eventually I start to feel loose, and then I go into whatever kind of training I had planned for that day. It's that simple.

I realize, however, that my casual ways are not ideal for everyone. Most serious walkers, including my daughter, believe in stretching exercises as a warmup. I admit that they are good for you even if I have never been able to discipline myself to do them regularly. With my daughter's help, I'll outline them for you and suggest that you do as I say, not as I do. (You may hate exercises too and will want to see if cheating on them works out as well for you as it has for me. The truth is that for all my avoidance of warmup exercises, I have escaped injuries through over a third of a century of competitive walking.)

Of course, there is another side to the exercise story. Through exercises, you can build strength effectively and make yourself a more flexible, faster walker. I know that I would have done better over the years if I had done such exercises. But I don't think I would have enjoyed my sport as much.

Anyway, your warmup exercises should aim at working every muscle in the body. A good one to start with is rolling your head around, stretching your neck and shoulder muscles. You drop your chin to your chest; then, holding down your shoulders, you roll your head so that your right ear is parallel to your right shoulder. Then you tip your head far back, get the left ear parallel to the left shoulder, and so on around in a circle. You can do this one either standing or sitting; just keep your spine straight.

One exercise you do not want to do is deep knee bends or squat jumps. Both of these often damage the legs instead of strengthening them. A halfway bend of the knees is all right, or you can get down with your hands and feet both on the ground. From this squatting position, straighten the legs, leaving the tips of your fingers on the ground.

Achilles Stretch

Perhaps the most standard stretching exercise before starting out is one in which you lean against a wall, tree, or post with your feet about three or four feet from the support. You do a sort of vertical pushup against the wall. Then, with one leg bent, you push the hips forward, stretching the calf and Achilles tendon of the other leg. Hold this position for ten to fifteen seconds. Be sure to use only gentle pressure on this or on any other stretching exercise.

Another simple Achilles stretch is to stand on a step with your heel hanging out in space beyond the step. Lower yourself with legs straight so that you feel the pull on the backs of your heels. Hold for ten seconds or so.

Windmill

The windmill exercise will get you limber. Extend your arms parallel to the ground and then alternately bend your body so that first your right hand touches the left toe, and then the left hand touches the right toe. Starting from the same position with arms outstretched, turn left, then right as far as possible, and this twisting action will get your midsection ready for the upcoming workout.

Woodchopper

The woodchopper is another good exercise. Standing with knees slightly bent, put your hands together, raise them over your head, and bend back so the hands go up and behind you. Then bring your hands forward and down, swinging them between your knees and reaching behind your feet to touch the ground.

Skipping Rope

Skipping rope without a rope will also bring a nicely balanced feeling of total body readiness for action. Simply go along in a skipping motion, swinging your arms to rotate the imaginary rope. Do it forward, sideways, and backwards for full benefit. (Like lots of exercises, this one basically looks ridiculous. You will probably want to do this in private. It also requires space. It's great on a track or in the woods, but not so good for right in front of your house with all the neighbors watching.)

Pushups

Although I'm a confessed calisthenics hater, for some reason I do like pushups. I go through periods during which I do pushups three or four times a day, only fifteen to twenty at a time, but still a formidable total during a month. Why I should like them and detest so many other exercises is a question for me and my psychiatrist (still nonexistent, I'm happy to say) to decide.

In any case, I have now listed all the exercises that I do myself with any regularity. Although I am too old to change my own ways, I feel that the least I can do is pass on the exercises my daughter Kate and others believe in. My suggestion to you is to work out your own program. Don't do them all at once. You would be spending more time stretching than walking if you did every one of these every day, but through trial and error, selection and rejection, you can come up with a choice of the following exercises that will prepare your body to walk in nearly total safety.

Breathe and Bend Backwards. This exercise will stretch the back and strengthen it. It will also stretch and strengthen the abdominal muscles and help to increase lung capacity.

1. Stand straight and raise your arms up high.
2. Breathe in deeply and push the hips forward as the back bends back.
3. Do this for ten seconds, then rest. Repeat three to five times.

Sitting Toe Touches. This exercise will stretch the backs of your legs. It gives you good control so you will not overdo but can slowly feel the muscles stretch and ease out.

1. Sit with your legs extended in front of you on the floor. Have your feet together.
2. Reach out and touch both toes at once, bringing your head as close to your knees as possible.
3. Repeat four to six times.

Bicycling. This one has been around for a long time, and it's still a good one for overall body flexibility.

1. Lie on your back and hoist your hips onto your hands, supporting your weight on your elbows under the body.
2. Pretend you're riding a bicycle upside down. Pump the bike with increasing vigor, reaching straight up toward the ceiling with your toes on each stride.
3. Do this for twenty to thirty cycles.

Note: Use common sense in all exercising. If bicycling or any other exercise is difficult for you, omit that exercise from your repertoire. These exercises are all designed as stretching and warmup activities, not as strength and dexterity tests. If you give up on an exercise because it's too difficult in the first month and then come back to it later and find you can do it easily, that's one of the nicest things about hard physical work. You reach certain points at which you have total proof that the program is doing something for you. So don't be discouraged when you can't do something; instead, think of that something as a future milestone that you are going to revel in passing.

Hurdler's Stretch. Hurdlers are athletes for whom body flexibility is as important as for walkers. This old standby obviously is designed to prepare a body to hurdle; it's also a good exercise for stretching many things at once.

1. Find a table, chair, or fence about three feet high and place one foot on the table so the knee is straight. The other leg reaches straight down to the floor.
2. Extend your fingers toward the toe on the table, keeping both legs straight. As you achieve full flexibility, you will be able to touch your forehead to your knee. (I never even came close, but most people can do it.)
3. Repeat twice with each leg.

Leg Split. This exercise holds benefits similar to the hurdler's stretch.

1. Sit with legs wide apart.
2. Reach out and take hold of one ankle with both hands.
3. Gently pull down your head toward your knee. Hold for a ten count.
4. Repeat three times with each leg.

Quadriceps Stretch. When you do this properly, you will feel the stretching at the upper part of the thigh. This exercise will help you increase your stride length.

1. Stand straight, balancing yourself with one hand against a chair or wall.
2. Bend your leg and grab your foot and hold it against your buttocks.
3. Gently push your knee back as far as it will go. Do the pushing with your leg, not with your hand. Hold for ten seconds.
4. Repeat twice with each leg.

Twist and Swing. This one will loosen the hips and shoulders.

1. Stand with feet about three feet apart. Hold your arms straight out horizontally.

   2. Twist your body at the waist, keeping the hips facing forward, and swing your arms, head, and body as far to one side as they will go.

   3. Repeat ten times to each side.

Windmill. This exercise will stretch the backs of the legs, the back, and the arms.

   1. Stand with feet apart, arms straight out at the sides.

   2. Bend forward at the waist so that your back is parallel to the floor, arms still spread out.

   3. Reach across and touch your left ankle with your right hand; then your right ankle with your left hand. Keep arms extended throughout the exercise. Do not rush your movements.

   4. Return to the erect position, arms still spread out.

   5. Repeat the cycle five times.

Arching. This exercise is good for upper body flexibility. It also stretches the hamstrings, calves, and ankles.

   1. Start on your hands and knees, head up, back flat. Slowly lower your head and arch your back.

   2. Curl your toes under your feet and straighten your legs, increasing the body's arch. Try to keep your feet flat on the floor.

   3. Hold for ten seconds. Repeat three times.

Situps. Of all the exercises I have disliked, situps lead the list. Still, there is no denying that they strengthen the middle regions or that, like medicine, they are good for you.

   1. Lie flat on your back with knees bent and hands clasped behind your head. It is helpful to brace your feet under a bureau, chair, or partner.

   2. Bring your body into a sitting position. Keep your back rounded.

   3. Touch your elbows to your knees, then return slowly to the starting position.

   4. Repeat ten times. (If you are aiming at strength, you can repeat many more than ten times, but ten is all I could bear to recommend.)

Back Stretch. Here's an easy one as a reward after you've done situps. Simply stand erect with your feet shoulder-width apart. Bend forward slowly at the waist and just hang there. Feel your arms, shoulders, and neck relax. You will feel a slight stretch at the backs of your legs, but that's all. When you come back up, bend your knees slightly to ease the pressure on your lower back.

Lying Relaxed. Here's another exercise for practice in relaxation, but it involves a bit more effort than the back stretch. If you do this one for ten minutes, you will be amazed at how good it makes you feel.

1. Lie on your back with your feet slightly spread, your arms not touching the body. Keep your palms up. Breathe deeply.
2. Lift your feet six inches off the floor. Hold for a ten count.
3. Relax.
4. Take a deep breath, hold it, and tighten every muscle in your body. Hold this as long as you can.
5. Then relax again, trying to feel that all your muscles are melting into a pool of softness. Lie there as long as you like, until you feel good, ready to take on any task.

Walking Exercises. These can be done as you move along on your training outings. The one I mentioned earlier about skipping rope without a rope is one. Here are two more, both of which will limber up your shoulders, arms, and waist and will help you to develop greater flexibility.

Moving Windmill. Swing your arms in backward circles as you stride along. It's as simple as that. Keep it up for 50 to 100 yards.

Clasped Hands Swing. Clasp your fingers together in front of you as you walk along. As you take a step to the right, pull both arms vigorously to the right side, then back and forth, the arms swinging to the side of the forward leg each stride. Do this one also for 50 to 100 yards (or simply take fifty strides if you have trouble estimating distances).

There is a final note about exercises, and that is that cooling down is as important as warming up and should not be neglected. If you do decide on an exercise program, make your selections by trial and error, rejecting the ones that are counterproductive for you. (By counterproductive, I mean either that the exercise is too difficult or too boring, the latter a long-term hazard because you simply are not going to keep on doing something that you dislike. As I have stated before, the key thing to your walking is to keep it pleasant so that it becomes a lifelong enjoyment for you, not just another thirty-day Magical Mystery Tour like all the diet things you read about in books and magazines.)

Real walking is so satisfactory that you don't have to try to fool yourself about it. That's going to be the secret of its long-term success.

5

What Are You Going to Gain?

If you are going to devote somewhere between three and ten hours a week to walking, hours taken from your precious free time, you want to know what's in it for you. What are you going to gain?

Well, for one thing, you're *not* going to gain weight. The dressing room before a walking race looks pretty much as though the inmates of a prisoner of war camp were gathering for some unusually happy event that has them all in smiles—although somewhat tense. That happiness cannot cover up the appearance that there is considerable malnutrition evident. Serious racewalkers are a scrawny lot.

Your goal probably is not to reduce yourself to the ultimate thinness of the great walker, but at least you can be pretty sure that you are going to lose weight and that the more you walk, the more you will lose.

On the other hand, there are still some pretty good walkers who aren't anywhere near scrawny. Ralph Cardarelli of the North Medford Club, for example, has cut his weight down from 240 to 180, but he is still pushing a rather large stomach around in his races. The weight hasn't stopped him from earning a national championship in the over-fifty age division of the 100-kilometer walk.

There are, however, many other physical benefits besides weight loss in walking. Most of us worry about heart attacks, for example. I know that every time I read about the symptoms of heart trouble, I usually manage to have a "heart attack" of some sort shortly afterwards. Pains in the arm and chest, shortness of breath, and so on have all bothered me at one time or another. Somehow, though, each attack has proved to be ephemeral, and I have survived nicely in spite of my imagination.

There are definite things that you have to watch out for if you want to avoid heart trouble (and who doesn't?). Blood pressure, weight, diet, cholesterol, pulse rate, mood, blood sugar, and a variety of technical things are all to be watched as part of the preventive side of avoiding heart attacks. Walking brings benefits in almost all of these areas.

Checking Cardiovascular Fitness

When you exercise hard, your heart pumps harder, faster. It adapts to the demands of the exercise, and gradually it becomes more efficient. There is no other way to cardiovascular fitness except through working your body hard enough to raise the pulse rate to a clearly defined level that benefits the heart. An easy stroll simply cannot do this, but racewalking will enable you to reach whatever pulse rate you are aiming for.

It is fairly well determined that the maximum heart beat rate for a human is around 220 beats per minute, and only young children can achieve that. As you age, your maximum beat rate goes down, roughly at the rate of one beat per year. Thus, a thirty-year-old will have a maximum of around 190 beats per minute, a fifty-year-old 170, and so on.

Since your goal is not to strain but to train, you should not be up near your maximum pulse beat during a workout. Somewhere around 75 percent is the ideal, so you have some simple math to do to figure out what your pulse rate should get up to during a good workout. Three-quarters of your theoretic maximum is your goal. If you are twenty years old with a maximum of 220 minus 20—or 200—the math is easy. You will be looking for a pulse rate of 150 (200 × 0.75).

Because there is a wide difference in heart beat rates among humans, the general range is worth knowing. Up to age twenty, your goal should be a pulse rate of between 150 and 180 beats per minute. In your twenties, a ten-beat drop to a 140 to 170 range is appropriate. It should be 130 to 160 in your thirties, 120 to 150 in your forties, 110 to 140 in your fifties, and 100 to 140 thereafter as the differences in human aging make it less and less sensible to try to set exact figures for the over-sixty athlete.

The way to determine your pulse rate is to count it immediately after stopping during a brisk workout. With a little practice, you will be able to find the beat on the inside of your wrist, your temple, or the carotid artery in your neck. You don't have to count for a whole minute. Fifteen seconds on your stop watch and then multiplying by four will give you the answer.

The thing about taking your pulse rate is that you learn two things. First, you know that you are working at a proper level and that you are safe from heart damage. Second, you may find that you really haven't reached the prescribed goal, and then you will feel free to pick up the tempo of your training, to work even harder. The main thing is that you won't have to worry, and you will know that you are benefiting your heart.

Early Morning Pulse Check

I also suggest taking your pulse lying in bed in the early morning. It's good practice for the mid-walk check. The beat is much more difficult to find when you are resting than when the old ticker is pounding away. But more than that, if you take your pulse rate regularly, you will find that it slows down very gradually as you get into shape. My daughter Kate, for example, was always athletic, but before she started serious distance training, her at-rest pulse rate was around sixty. After a year, she was ten beats per minute slower. Obviously, if your heart is doing the same work with fewer beats per minute, that heart is working more easily, and you have the statistical proof that all your miles have done something for you.

Now, I hope I haven't made too big a thing of this pulse counting. Actually, I don't think I interrupt a workout more than half a dozen times a year to do this. Still, after so many years of running and racewalking, I am much more certain of the durability of my heart than most people can afford to be, so I really do recommend the stop-and-count method for most beginners. It's a good expenditure of fifteen seconds. However, I hope that no one becomes a slave to the pulse beat count and does it all the time, making every workout revolve around a series of fifteen-second countdowns. Always remember to use a good dose of common sense in coaching yourself.

Dr. Sheehan on Walking

Although the heart may be the chief beneficiary of racewalking, the whole body gains in a variety of other ways. Dr. George Sheehan has written innumerable books extolling the wonders of running. He is a good runner himself, and as a doctor he knows the body intimately. In his book *Dr. Sheehan on Running*, he devotes two of the 204 pages to comments on racewalking. Among the things he concedes are these:

> The racewalker, for one thing, can make do with ordinary feet. He can put miles and miles on feet that would break down in any other sport.
>
> The main source of this protection is the walker's swivel-hipped form. . . . His foot plant—starting with the heel, riding along the outside of the foot and delivering straight ahead—is just what the Creator planned. And the locked knee, a racewalking requirement, keeps the kneecap in its appropriate place, the patellar groove, thus preventing the too-frequent knee problems seen in runners, tennis players, and other athletes.
>
> Why this form also wards off sciatica is more difficult to explain . . . Whatever the reason, sciatica is almost unheard of in racewalkers. And some who took up the sport in the throes of sciatic symptoms have had rapid cures once they started striding through their neighborhoods.
>
> Indeed, racewalking is a safe refuge for any injured athlete. It is the perfect sport for recuperating from some other sport.

Of course, I would go one step beyond Dr. Sheehan and suggest that racewalking is the perfect sport to switch to permanently, not just to take up from time to time when your regular activity cripples you.

So the answer to the question as to what you can gain from taking up racewalking is a simple one: From head to toe and all points in between, you will be better off. Even the worst feet will thrive when you racewalk. Your legs will firm up and slim down, and the knees, the most vulnerable part, will be safe. Your waist will grow smaller, your stomach flatter and stronger. Your heart will be safe as it grows stronger. Your upper arms will no longer be flabby. And your head will benefit from all of this because you will feel better. You can't help feeling better because you will be better.

It's a great feeling, and it's yours for a small investment of time. Step right up, ladies and gentlemen, and take advantage of this amazing, all-through-a-lifetime offer!

6

What Can You Lose?

L et's face it: Many of you are thinking of walking out of desperation, not out of love of sports. You looked at yourself naked in the mirror, and the bulging middle, the thick thighs, the extra chins, the overall flabby look was so depressing that you vowed to do something about it. Now you are hoping that walking can be that something.

Well, you really can't lose anything except weight by taking up walking. It won't automatically get you into a Miss America contest (or even into your old high school clothes), but it is going to help. You'll still find people with big midsections competing in walking races, but as a general rule even the stouter ones will have lost weight through walking.

As in any diet or exercise program, the trouble with weight control through walking is that the mathematics are simple, but the self-discipline is complicated. One year my friend Bob Morse walked over 2,000 carefully charted miles. Yet when he went to a new doctor for a physical, the doctor recommended that although Bob was reasonably fit, he should "take up more exercise to get rid of some weight." The exercise Bob needed was one of mental discipline. He loved ice cream and often single-handedly destroyed a half gallon in an evening. I should also add that a year after that physical, when he was in much the same weight bracket, he won the over-forty national title in a two-mile walk at Tufts University.

The way you lose weight through walking is to use up more calories than you consume. If, for example, you have settled into a steady weight pattern and can control your eating so you remain at that level, a program of walking that is combined with the same eating habits will bring you down on the weight scale by slow but definite degrees.

The goal for all people should be what they weighed at the age of twenty (assuming, of course, that you were not already overweight at that age). After a year of walking, you can expect to lose between ten and fifty pounds, depending on how much extra weight you have to start with and how often you get out and walk fast.

One thing that is going to help you will be the athlete's attitude that you develop by becoming a walker. The big spur to successful dieting is incentive, and I can tell you that the desire to walk better is a great incentive to better eating habits. I can use myself as an example. I am naturally thin. My father was killed in an accident when he was 67, and although he was not particularly athletic, all his clothes fit me. We were both around 5'8" and 140 pounds. So I don't need to diet, and furthermore I have a stomach that seems able to handle anything except alcohol. I love butter, cream, sweets, fats, fried foods, and all the things that are bad for you. And yet, with no incentive for good diet other than wanting to race better, I have modified my intake of desserts and candy, and I eat quite a sensible diet now.

For the person with a need to lose weight, that added incentive of wanting to walk better can be the thing that tips the scales in favor of more sensible eating.

Here is the basic mathematical information you need to set up a sensible diet for yourself. Everything depends on calories, and the calorie is a unit of measurement of energy produced by food and oxidized by the body. The calories not burned up by exercise are stored as fat. (Ironically, this means that a body like mine, which does not store up much fat, is quite inefficient. I can eat fattening foods and waste most of the excess, whereas the efficient body of the fat person turns every extra calorie into fat. In a society less lavish in its food supplies than ours, the person with the ability to get a great deal out of very little food would be the one more likely to survive.)

Anyway, an extra 3,500 calories taken into the system as excess baggage will be a pound of fat. Similarly, 3,500 calories used up in excess over what you ate that day will equal a pound of fat lost. As calories get burned up by walking, just as in any exercise, you can see that enough miles will get you down on the weight scale.

On most diet charts walking is rated low as a way of burning up calories. That's because they are talking about strolling, not fast walking. The truth is that the painfully slow jogger, the one taking twelve minutes to cover a mile, will burn up fewer calories than the walker covering ground at the same pace. Racewalking at a twelve-minute-a-mile pace will burn off roughly 500 to 550 calories. Thus, walking seven miles could cause you to lose a pound.

At ten minutes a mile, the benefits from walking are greater: 700 to 750 calories are burned per mile of racewalking or about 150 more calories per mile than jogging at the same pace would burn off.

Thus, when studying caloric burn charts you must remember that most of those charts are talking about ordinary walking, not racewalking. Professor Robert Guitin of Columbia University was the first to discover that racewalking at jogging speeds burned more calories than running at the same speed. The discovery is hardly surprising, however, when you consider the extra energy that your upper body expends in walking as compared to running.

Thus, you can walk with the satisfying knowledge that it is a fine aerobic exercise, giving you all the benefits of any strenuous exercise without the accompanying detriments of other forms of exercise.

It almost goes without saying that those who start walking for reasons other than weight control, those who already are the right shape, even if they are not really in good shape, will have an extra pleasure in their eating and will find that they can actually eat more, enjoy meals more, and still remain the same satisfying shape while they also are getting into good shape in the other sense of the word. (Going back to Bob Morse, it is obvious that his half-gallon-of-ice-cream habit would have made him a blimp if he had not been putting in those forty miles a week. He literally paid for his ice-cream habit by his almost equally pleasurable walking habit.)

Unless you are amazingly sales resistant or thin, you must have read one of the myriad diet books or magazine articles and you have probably experimented with a diet based on bananas, rice, fruits, water, nuts, yogurt or on just about any food that will get you alternately bored and frantic as you persist on the diet.

Diets don't lose weight for you. Mental discipline does. Walking is a way to develop mental discipline, and, in terms of eating, to make that discipline easier because you can eat as much as you ever did and still lose weight.

But don't take my word for it. Find a walker and talk to him or her about the subject of weight. We are almost all practically messianic about our sport, and the real person you talk to will be far more convincing than any parade of famous characters that I could offer on these pages.

As with everything else about walking, in the matter of diet you are your own coach. I am not going to set up an ideal week, month, or year of eating for you to follow. All you need is certain principles and your own good sense and determination.

Let's start by telling you that the average American diet contains around 40 percent fat. The American Heart Association recommends a diet of no more than 35 percent fat. Some extreme diets get the fat content as low as 10 percent, and that's great if you like the food, but I am advocating walking for the normal, pleasure-seeking person, not for the fanatics. (I'm not being sarcastic. I really admire the fanatics, but because they love going to extremes, they tend to think that fanaticism is for everyone. My theory is that normal, easy-going people can gain 90 percent of the benefits of fanaticism and still maintain a happy, normal life.)

Remember that eating, along with sex and sleeping, is one of the truly great pleasures of life. Don't ruin that pleasure. Walking should make it even keener.

I suggest three ways for the walker to approach eating. The first is the way for the favored sons and daughters, the ones who can eat just about anything at any time and still remain thin, the ones with inefficient systems that simply waste too many calories to let the body get fat. They should eat for enjoyment and temper that enjoyment with common sense, avoiding a steady diet of junk food, rich food, and indecent gorging in front of their dieting friends and family. Eat for good health. Cut down on chocolate bars a bit. Enjoy your meals, but don't abuse the privilege. For you, the path is an easy one.

The second path is for those who have already come to grips with their weight. You are ten pounds overweight (or twenty or fifty) but you haven't changed in ages. You know how much you can eat; you have been eating that amount for years. Now all you have to do is start walking. If you keep on eating the same as before, you obviously won't gain weight through walking, and gradually you will find that burning off those 500-plus calories every mile eventually will knock off the pounds. It may take a year to lose ten pounds, but, as I have already said, the mathematics are simple. The extra exercise will knock off weight as long as the intake of calories remains less than what you use up.

The third path is for the problem group, those who are still gaining weight, who have never before succeeded in a permanent weight loss, who have tried every diet and failed to lose weight and keep it off, who are unhappy about their weight problem.

I think I should pause here and speak to the women dieters among my readers. You are the victims of a male chauvinist society that has made you unhappy with your beauty even when it is truly breathtaking. If Venus herself were walking the earth today, the magazines and TV shows would crush her spirit and send her off to a sauna to steam off a good percentage of that gorgeous body. I have heard many high school girls complain about their "weight problem." To me, they have looked wonderful. It bothers me to have a naturally chunky, attractive young woman speak of her dislike of her body, of her need to be thinner.

I guess my message to most women is to think in terms of strength, not thinness. Get in good athletic shape, and let your looks take care of themselves. An interesting sidelight to this is the outcome of several studies, all of which indicate that athletic women, women who are in top shape, are "better" sexually than flabbier women. In other words, good condition is as feminine as it is masculine, and as you would not, I suppose, want a pudgy, weak lover, neither should you want to be an out-of-shape loved one yourself.

Weight Reduction Checklist

But, back to my advice to my third group of readers, the ones who need help in losing weight. Here are some recommendations that should help.

1. Count your calories.

2. Eat the standard, balanced diet that all nutritionists agree on. Don't go in for fad diets. Include green vegetables, fruit, cheeses and milk, whole-grain bread and cereals, potatoes, and lean meat and fish in your diet. Go easy on butter and cream.

3. Avoid fried foods. My friend Johnny Kelley, the famed marathoner now well into his seventies, still competes successfully, beating about half the field in any race, and he has never been on a diet of any sort. "I eat what my good wife, Laura, sets before me," Johnny has told me, "but we don't have fried foods." That is truly good advice. Frying food increases the calorie count and makes the food harder to digest.

4. Cut down on your sugar intake. The average American eats 100 pounds of sugar a year, two pounds every week. That's about a pound of body fat every week. Sugar is in everything, and it is not

doing you much good (much as I hate to write such things about something I love). You don't have to cut it out, but cutting down does make you feel better, I have to admit. Use fresh fruit instead of canned—a great excuse for eating something expensive but delicious! Choose your cereals carefully. Take your coffee and tea without sugar. Eat half as much candy as you are now consuming, ditto with desserts, substituting fresh fruit a few times a week. Skip the next trip to the ice cream shop.

5. Treat salt as you do sugar. It is in so many products that you can't avoid it, but you can cut down on the amount you sprinkle on your food and on the amount that you cook with in your house. You don't have to give it up, but you can certainly cut down and that will help.

6. Learn how good water is. It has fewer calories than Tab, Diet Pepsi, or anything. If you don't feel right about drinking something that's almost free, shell out a bundle for Perrier or some such thing, but rediscover water. I lived in Mississippi for a few weeks one summer, and our well was contaminated by the outhouse. We had to boil all our water and then cool it. There were a dozen of us living in one house, and we had little organization. As a result, we drank soft drinks to quench our thirst most of the time. I can tell you that water suddenly came to seem like the greatest drink the world has ever known, and of course, that is exactly what it is. Drink water!

7. Keep a firm control over your caloric intake, and plan ahead for a special meal—that is, eat fewer calories for a couple of days before dining out at a good restaurant. Then you won't feel guilty about eating well. And remember that eating well should refer to quality, not quantity.

In general, as far as your dieting goes, it should be as natural and unforced as possible. You can use the naughty foods you love as a reward for extra workouts. If you walk an unplanned five miles on what was scheduled to be your day off, you can reward yourself with dessert or a nice fat lamb chop. Use the "carrot-or-stick" approach to motivating yourself. If you've been lazy that day, eat a carrot; if you worked extra hard, buy yourself an ice cream on a stick.

But above all be normal about your eating. Don't make yourself miserable. Remember that you are setting a pattern for a lifetime, and the only way it is going to stick is if you learn to enjoy it.

Keep in mind that you are an athlete. Instead of the Olympics, your goal is to beat the former you. Whatever you do today is to be measured against yesterday. When you win that one, you then go to work on another tomorrow in which you will be out to defeat the present you.

Get caught up in the excitement of creating a more athletic you. Keep written records of time for a mile, times and repetitions for an interval workout, and keep notes on your weight. Weigh yourself at the same time of day, preferably morning, and weigh yourself in the nude. Then you will know that any change is fairly valid, and that you may properly celebrate a lost pound. After all, pounds are all you're going to lose by walking; otherwise, you can only win.

7

How Often Should You Train?

There is no part of a walking program in which you are more the sole arbiter of what is correct than in deciding what your training schedule should be. A book can set up lovely neat schedules, but it can't take into account the variety of things that interrupt your life. Neither can it determine the level of desire and eagerness that you have.

If I were to set arbitrary times, distances, and frequency of training, I easily could put down the average ideal. But just as you would hate to raise the half child of the average two-and-a-half-child family, so too you would probably hate my ideal schedule.

Thus, instead of saying that you should do such and such on Mondays, so and so on Tuesdays, and the like, I will give you some principles on which to build your own program and then offer some sample schedules that could work for you.

The most important thing about a schedule is that once you set it up you must follow it. I have known remarkably untalented bodies whose owners took them out for a daily workout 365 days of the year regardless of weather. Such dedication always pays off. I also have known some strong, athletic types who start their training with a world of enthusiasm but with the idea that they love walking (or running) so much that they know they are going to *want* to get out *almost* every day. They feel they don't need schedules, which would crush their free spirits and enthusiasm.

Well, such people are like my former writing students who could only create when the spirit moved them. They couldn't be bothered with my assignments because such a dull approach might kill their creative spark. I know that such a creative spirit may exist somewhere, but in my years of teaching writing, I found that good writers can settle down to the task and do it without regard for their more tender feelings. It is the same with walking. If you go out only when you feel like it, you won't get far.

This is especially true for those of you who follow my early-morning walk schedule. I have never really loved my workouts, at least not compared to a final half hour's extra sleep in the morning. To get out of bed, I have to work on myself psychologically. It's not easy, and I can't afford to let my lazy side have any advantage.

The best part is that once I manage to get in motion, I am almost always glad I did. I may feel stiff, tired, and unhappy for the first half mile, but soon the body finds its rhythm, and I am delighted with the world once again. I am a morning person anyway. One reason I walk is to keep away from my wife, who is a morning grouch. She doesn't want me around with my cheery chatter, so I go out walking with the dogs and we are both better off for it. For Mary to adopt an early morning training schedule would be fatal—fatal to any possibility of success. She would hate it, and as I have said before, if you can't find ways of making your training satisfactory, you are not going to stick with it very long.

The second thing about your schedule is that it must be flexible enough to cover all situations. For example, if you live, as I do, where it rains often, you have to decide whether you are going to be an all-weather or fair-weather walker. I recommend the all-weather approach because I like to show off, and if your friends see you trudging through a driving rain, they are going to be impressed— either by your determination or by your mental deterioration.

On the other hand, if your feet blister easily, if you tend to catch heavy colds, if you have only one pair of shoes, or if you just plain hate the discomfort of being wet, you are going to want to avoid the rain.

One thing you can do is search out an indoor walking area. Any building that will permit you to walk fifty paces will do—along school corridors, in the hallways of large offices, gymnasiums, theaters, warehouses, and so on. At dawn, all you need is someone (probably a watchman) who will let you in and then ignore you. There won't be many others around to bother you.

One thing that helps me to get going is my dogs. They love to run. Fixed females, their interests in life center on food, sleep, and walks. Their limited vocabularies start and end with "eat," "run," and "walk." All three words send them into paroxysms of joy. Their enjoyment of the outings helps me to realize that walking really is fun and that I am not weird to be doing it.

By experimentation, you will learn just how often your body and spirit can stand to work out. That is the proper amount for you. If you are so tired from one workout that you can't do anything the next, your body is being overworked. If you find you are dreading the grind of a daily outing, that you would almost welcome an accident to break the awful pattern, then your spirit is rebelling and you're trying too much.

Common sense tells you that if you can't get out at least twice a week, you are kidding yourself if you think walking is going to do you any good. The one exception is the person in a physically demanding job who can take a two-hour workout on Sundays. That person is strong to begin with, is working all week on other exercise, and can concentrate on technique in that one workout. Such people usually don't have time to read books like this one, however.

The Right Distance

I recommend that your early schedule be based on an every-other-day workout to begin with, and that your own experience will tell you if you can boost this to a daily workout. There will be those, however, who will find that two or three short walks a day are more convenient and effective than one harder one. For example, if you live the right distance from work and can change clothes at work, walking is the finest transportation of all. That is how I went to school the last three or four years I was teaching. It made for a good workout and cost me little in time. Not everyone, however, ends up at work and finds a hot shower waiting there.

The "right distance" for a workout will be up to you to determine. Time, not distance, is the best measuring device. You can get good benefits from a fifteen-minute workout, and you can go for three hours a day if your body can stand it. The decisions as to what to do each day must be made by you.

The Three Improvement Factors

There are three factors involved in your improvement as a walker. First of all, there is how fast you walk, then how far you walk, and finally how much rest you take between walks. The great walkers can go over 100 miles a day and maintain that for several days. Others are straining after one mile.

Your goal is to improve. Thus, you must find out where to start. That means that you must first time yourself on a track or some other measured course. Next you must find out how much stamina you have. Do this in as pleasant a way as possible. Devote a Saturday or Sunday to taking a really long walk you have always meant to do—from one town to the next, around a beautiful area, or exploring a city. Walk for a couple of hours, rest, and snack. Then walk another two hours. If you can handle more than four hours of walking, do so. Without being a fanatic, test out where your limits lie. Then find out how long you have to rest after such a long walk. Three days of rest should be enough.

Interval Training

Your daily workouts also will involve the same three factors of speed, distance, and rest. The basis of interval training is handling these three things in such a way that you are constantly improving. That is why I suggest a minimum of twice a month in interval work on a track or other carefully measured quarter mile.

Let's say you're at the bottom of the fitness barrel, and it takes you sixteen minutes of hard work to go one mile. That's four minutes for each time around the track, so if you do only one lap and do it in three minutes forty-five seconds, you are speeding up. Set 3:45 as your quarter-mile pace. Do it once and then slow down to a stroll, as slowly as necessary for you to regain your strength. When you feel better, do another 3:45 quarter. Maybe you will be able to do only three such repetitions. In your record book (if you are the type who enjoys keeping records as I do), put down "3 × 3:45, one lap stroll in between."

The next time you go out, either aim at a faster pace (3:40 to 3:44), more repetitions (but never increase by more than one at a time), or a shorter rest period, perhaps only 400 yards instead of the whole 440-yard lap.

Since one rule of an interval workout is to stop while you still feel you could do one more, improvement should be possible without serious strain. Another rule is that if you are straining to accomplish any workout, stay at that level for a while until it begins to get easier.

One thing you must do very early in your self-coaching career is to analyze yourself psychologically. If you are a creative, poetic type, you can probably ruin your training by doing everything on the track, timing and measuring each day's effort, and keeping scientific track of your progress. Such an approach may be perfect for the mathematical walker, but for artistic you there are better ways.

Fartlek

Fartlek, a Swedish term that runners have used for years, gives the same benefits as interval training on a track. I've been told the term means "speed play" (it also means lots of giggles when you suggest it to a high school track team), and in fartlek you do play with speed. On your workout you walk at various speeds, somewhat as the spirit moves you, going absolutely all out for a short stretch, slowing to a recovery stroll for as long as necessary, pretending you are in a race and maintaining a good, controlled pace for a while, playing any games with speed that you can devise as you move along.

Whether in interval training, fartlek, or a race, you must at times strive to go faster than you usually do. Your schedule should plan for this. If you go out and do exactly the same thing every day—let's say five miles at a fairly brisk pace—you will soon reach a level and stay there. But if you are working on a variety of speeds and distances, your body will adapt to the demands of several kinds of walking challenges, and like a champion you will find yourself getting better.

Your Chief Competition

I know that not all people are as competitive as I am, but I also know that everyone has the same chief rival that I do, and that's yourself. Whether you get great satisfaction from beating others or hate competition, you should be chiefly concerned with beating yourself.

By that, I mean that you should keep written or mental notes on what you were able to do yesterday and then go out today and beat yesterday's mark. At my age and with so many efforts behind me when I was younger and stronger, it is hard for me to score an all-time victory over myself, but frequently I can manage a new record for recent years. For example, just today I left the car at work for my wife and timed myself on the four-mile trek home. Halfway through I felt good, glanced at my watch, and saw that I was doing well. That encouraged me to pick up the pace, and I finished thirty seconds faster than I had ever done before, and I have been covering that stretch off and on for four years now. I felt mildly euphoric after that outing, and that little touch of euphoria is part of one of the best things about getting in shape—setting personal records.

The nicest thing about personal competition with oneself is that those who start out in the worst shape, those who are the least competitive, have the best self-improvement opportunities.

One Schedule

Getting back to schedules, I will put together a few examples, not for you to follow slavishly but for you to judge your own schedules by. Maybe I should start with my own, not as something anyone else would follow but as a way of telling you just how individualistic a schedule can be.

I get up five days a week and take an easy workout with my dogs. I try to do it before it is too light out because my neighbors are somewhat less than enamored of my three dogs; as long as the neighbors are sleeping, however, they don't know that the dogs have been around (they may suspect it, however). I go about five miles during each of these five days, walking medium hard on two, walking and jogging as the spirit moves me on two others, and running most of the way on the fifth. On one of the other two days I either race against my own times on a four-mile course or I enter a race—usually ten kilometers. The seventh workout, Sunday mornings, is with a group of friends who gather regularly, and this is my toughest workout, seven miles of fairly hard running.

Thus, you can see that I am doing about forty miles a week (less than I'd recommended to someone else aiming at the goals I have). I run about as much as I walk, partly because it doesn't take as long, partly because my friends are runners, not walkers, and mostly because the races on Cape Cod are usually running and I love races so I have to practice for what is available.

You also will notice that I don't do any interval work. I know that I should do it, and I really plan to get serious sometime and do my intervals, but at this particular moment I must admit that I haven't done any interval training—not on a regular basis anyway—for close to two years now.

What follows are three more practical schedules for the beginner to study when planning his or her own. One is for an out-of-shape beginner with limited time to spare. The second is for another beginner, one who has decided to work at the sport seriously, putting in all the time necessary. The third is for the in-shape person who wants to improve rapidly and then stay in top shape.

If you want to train "properly," any one of these three schedules will do just fine to give you a ten-week program. After that, you may either sustain the work of the final weeks, or you may move on to ten more planned weeks at a more challenging level, or, most likely, you will have enough feeling for making a schedule to go on and build one that fits your own unique needs.

Planning Your Own Schedule

Most of you will want to plan your own schedule right from the start. In that case, the three sample schedules will serve as general guidelines, and you will make your own changes, additions, and deletions as needed.

Even for the person who really likes to follow a pattern of proven success, the three schedules below should be modified by common sense. For example, if you go out and walk quite easily on the Easy Beginner schedule, and you find that you naturally take 130 steps each minute, don't slow down. Simply step up all the requirements on the schedule to match what you can do. The same holds true for those who find the standards too stiff. If you try your first fifteen to sixteen minute timed mile in the fourth week and find it takes you seventeen minutes, don't despair; simply rewrite all your schedules for a minute or a minute and a half more than the book says. Don't worry; soon you will be walking at the pace you've aimed at for a goal. It's just that it takes some bodies longer to achieve things than it takes others.

8

Three Schedules

*E**ach of these schedules* is laid out for a ten-week period. As the three dovetail into one another, you could follow this schedule for at least thirty weeks—and probably more because for any week or two-week period in which you find yourself struggling to meet the standards, you should repeat that week a third or fourth time until you feel confident about advancing.

To keep the schedules brief, I will use certain terms and abbreviations. Here's an explanation of them:

RW is racewalking, meaning that you concentrate on your style, monitoring it carefully and selecting one aspect to concentrate on that day.

In form also means racewalking, but it is to be done in a carefree manner, breezing along, worrying about nothing. "In-form" days are your reward for working hard on other days.

INT means interval work and refers to the chart in the chapter after this one. In interval work you walk a given distance, usually a quarter mile, and repeat that distance anywhere from three to twenty times, taking a rest interval between efforts. The rest interval is usually the same distance as the speed work, but as you advance on the chart, you may be able to cut your rest period to half the distance of the speed stuff.

Fartlek means "speed play." In a fartlek workout, you omit timed intervals, but walk at varying speeds. For example, in an hour and a half fartlek workout you might start with a mile or so of slow work in form. Then for the rest of the time you would alternate these slow in-form periods with varying bursts of racewalk effort, including 50 to 100 yards at near maximum, 50 to 100 yards at absolute maximum, up to a half mile of the race pace you wish were yours, plus hard uphill and downhill work as the terrain dictates. It doesn't matter what order you do things in. Remember that you are playing around with speed in this workout.

Stroll means to walk comfortably, slow enough so you feel less tired. Feel free to stop and look at nature while strolling.

PS means pleasant surroundings. When you take a PS workout, you are supposed to enjoy it, and a wooded area, a country road, a beach, or a park can contribute to this feeling of pleasure. PS also can mean that you find some kindred pleasant souls to accompany you on these outings.

Mi., *Min.*, and *Hr.* mean mile, minute, and hour. Thus, "3 mi. RW at 15–16 min." means you should go three miles, with each mile taking you between fifteen and sixteen minutes.

Besides deciding on a place to walk, you also must consider the time of day you are going to do it. Be realistic. If you're an evening person who has never been able to do anything well in the early morning, don't expect walking to change you. Morning is perhaps the best time to walk, but later morning—if your work permits—noon hour, or late afternoon (ideal for students and teachers) all have their advantages. Evening workouts are usually possible for everyone but are the least desirable because of the dangers of traffic and twisted ankles. Most people like to train at approximately the same time each day, but I've always found that variety helps, and I walk at all hours.

In choosing a time, try to avoid giving up anything else. Don't make a martyr of yourself. Remember that walking is fun. Add it to your day in a way that figures to increase your pleasure, not to rob you of the enjoyment of something else. Your family and friends will appreciate your not spoiling other activities.

You should start your regular walks a week or two before you embark on the schedules below. During this period, simply get used to getting out of the house and walking—not in racewalking style, but in your regular walk. This will do two things for you: It will get your body used to walking three or more times a week as serious exercise, and it will serve to tell you whether or not the times you have chosen are suitable. These preschedule walks should last about thirty to forty-five minutes and should be as brisk as you can make them without feeling any strain.

I have named my schedules Easy Beginner, Advanced Beginner, and Competitive Rookie. None of them demands any knowledge of training methods on your part. All can be followed easily. I expect those who take the Easy Beginner way to be in the large majority. Such walkers have little present conditioning; they are not fanatical about getting into competition in a hurry; and they want to spend a minimum amount of time in their new venture. An Easy Beginner should be ready for the advanced training in about three months. Admitting that you are an Easy Beginner doesn't mean that you have decided never to get good, merely that you recognize that you aren't in good shape yet.

The Advanced Beginner is still fairly easy. No matter how inexperienced you are, if you time yourself for a practice mile and find you can do it easily in fifteen minutes or less, you are already able to handle the Advanced Beginner workouts. That is, you are ready if you can afford to devote the extra time necessary in comparison to the Easy Beginner schedule. The quickest way to tell if you are ready for the Advanced Beginner work is to count your steps for a minute of real walking. If you are near 130 steps or higher, you should not have much trouble with the more challenging beginner work.

The Competitive Rookie is for those who take up the sport when they are already in pretty good shape. These people, most of whom will be dissatisfied runners, will be able to walk three miles in forty to forty-two minutes even though their style won't be very smooth. On the improvement chart, they will be able to handle six or more intervals at approximately three minutes per quarter mile. Competitive Rookie status also means that you are just about ready to try your walking skills in a real race.

Okay, then, here are the schedules:

FIRST AND SECOND WEEKS

	Easy Beginner	Advanced Beginner	Competitive Rookie
Sunday	RW 90–100 steps per minute for 30 min.	RW one mi. at 14–15 min. Stroll one mi. Then RW a second mi. in 14–15 min.	RW 3 mi. at 13–14 min. pace.
Monday	Rest.	Rest.	One mi. at 13–14 min. Stroll a mi. to res Then one more mi. a 13–14 min. pace.

	Easy Beginner	Advanced Beginner	Competitive Rookie
Tuesday	In form for 30 min.	2 mi. at 14–15 min. pace.	3 mi. at 13–14 min. pace.
Wednesday	Rest.	INT. (For your first interval workout, follow the directions in the next chapter [Improvement Chart] to find out where you should start on the chart.)	INT.
Thursday	30 min. In form at 90–120 steps per min.	Fartlek, 30 min.	Fartlek, 1 hr.
Friday	Rest.	Rest.	In form, 1 hr.
Saturday	Stroll 1 hr.	RW 3 mi., 14–15 min. pace.	RW 5 mi., 13—14 min. pace.

THIRD WEEK

The first two weeks were a kind of shake-down cruise. You began the base on which you will build all your future strength, stamina, and speed. In this third week, you will continue to build up that base (ten miles for the Easy Beginner, fifteen for the Advanced Beginner, and close to thirty for the Competitive Rookie). You will also take your first step toward improved quality of walking.

Of course, along with this schedule you must be working on style. Think about what your arms are doing; have your partner check you for angle of foot plant, straightening of the leg, closeness of arms to body, and so on. Partners should make these checks when the other is not aware that the observation is going on. In other words, monitor each other throughout RW workouts.

	Easy Beginner	Advanced Beginner	Competitive Rookie
Sunday	RW for 30 min. at 105–125 steps per min.	RW 3 mi. at 14–15 min. pace.	In form for 1 to 1½ hr.
Monday	Rest.	Rest.	RW 3 mi., 13–14 min. pace.
Tuesday	RW 45 min. at 100–120 steps per min.	RW 1 mi. at 14–15 min. pace. Stroll 1 mi. RW 1 mi. at 14–15 min. pace.	RW 4 mi. at 13–14 min. pace.
Wednesday	Rest.	INT. Advance one step on Improvement Chart.	INT. Advance one step on Improvement Chart.

	Easy Beginner	*Advanced Beginner*	*Competitive Rookie*
Thursday	INT. Find your place on the Improvement Chart.	Fartlek, 40 min.	Fartlek, 1 hr.
Friday	Rest.	Rest.	RW 3 mi. at 13–14 min. pace.
Saturday	RW for 45 min. at 105–125 steps per min.	PS in form, 1 hr.	PS in form, 2 hr.

FOURTH AND FIFTH WEEKS

The Easy Beginner increases distance gradually to about twelve miles for the week. The Advanced Beginner and the Competitive Rookie both make big moves this week, dropping a day of rest from each schedule. If you find that the improvement expected is more than you can handle easily, don't hesitate to keep that day of rest at least through the fourth week and possibly more. It's perfectly all right to take six, seven, or more weeks to get through these five weeks. In fact, the only danger is trying to shortcut the weeks—spending one week on this phase, for example, instead of two. As long as you are thinking in terms of long-term benefits and know that you're going to be doing this for a long, long time, you won't feel any ego pressure to try more than is called for. Trust the schedule. It will work.

	Easy Beginner	*Advanced Beginner*	*Competitive Rookie*
Sunday	PS in form, 1 hr.	RW 3 mi. at 14–15 pace.	RW 2 mi. at 12–13 min pace.
Monday	Rest.	In form, 1 hr.	RW 5 mi. at 13–15 pace.
Tuesday	RW 3 mi. at 15–16 min. pace.	INT.	INT.
Wednesday	Rest.	RW 3 mi. at 14–15 min. pace.	RW 4 mi. at 12.5–14 min. pace.
Thursday	INT.	Fartlek, 1 hr.	Fartlek, 1 hr.
Friday	Rest.	Rest.	RW 3 mi. at 13–15 min. pace.
Saturday	RW 4 mi. at 15–16 min. pace.	PS in form, 1 hr.	PS in form, 2 hr.

SIXTH AND SEVENTH WEEKS

The Easy Beginners drop one of their rest days this week. (But if the maximum time you can allow for training is four days a week, keep the Wednesday rest and simply take more than two weeks to complete the suggested sessions for this period.) The Easy Beginners are now up to about fifteen miles a week, the Advanced Beginners to about twenty, and the Competitive Rookies to around thirty-five miles for the week.

	Easy Beginner	*Advanced Beginner*	*Competitive Rookie*
Sunday	RW 4 mi. at 15–16 min. pace.	RW 3 mi. at 14–15 min. pace.	PS Stroll, 2 hr.
Monday	Rest.	In form, 1 hr.	RW 4 mi. at 13–14 min. pace.
Tuesday	RW 2 mi. at 14–15 min. pace.	RW 4 mi. at 14–15 min. pace.	RW 1 mi. in 12 min. Stroll 1 mi. RW 1 mi. in 12 min.
Wednesday	INT.	INT.	INT.
Thursday	RW 1 mi. in 13–14 min. Stroll 1 mi. RW 1 mi. in 13–14 min.	Fartlek, 1 hr.	Fartlek, 1 hr.
Friday	Rest.	Rest.	In form, 1 hr.
Saturday	RW 3 mi. at 14–15 min. pace.	RW 5 mi. at 14–15 min. pace.	RW 3 mi. at 12–13 min. pace.

EIGHTH WEEK

This week's schedule is aimed mainly at boosting your weekly total mileage a bit. The three weeks from six through eight are designed to give you the basis for the final push of weeks nine and ten to let you get the feel of how easy it is to advance your training as long as you keep the improvement increments very small. If you keep notes on how you feel during these final weeks, you will be in a position to set up your own schedule for weeks eleven through infinity, or until you quit, whichever comes first.

	Easy Beginner	*Advanced Beginner*	*Competitive Rookie*
Sunday	In form, 1 hr.	In form, 1½ hr.	RW 4 mi. at 13–14 min. pace.
Monday	Rest.	RW 3 mi. at 13–14 min. pace.	RW 3 mi. at 12–13 min. pace.
Tuesday	RW 3 mi. at 14–15 min. pace.	RW 5 mi. at 14–15 min. pace.	RW 5 mi. at 13–14 min. pace.
Wednesday	INT.	INT.	INT.
Thursday	RW 2 mi. at 13–14 min. pace.	Fartlek, 1 hr.	Fartlek, 1½ hr.
Friday	Rest.	Rest.	RW 4 mi. at 14–15 min. pace.
Saturday	RW 4 mi. at 14–15 min. pace.	RW 4 mi. at 13–14 min. pace.	PS in form for 2 hr.

NINTH AND TENTH WEEKS

These weeks are normal steps for the two beginners because each of them can move along to the next ten-week schedule. For the Competitive Rookie, however, these final two weeks are your first big test. The steps from last week to this are giant ones. If you can handle them easily, it means you have a firm base for all your future training. I would suggest that you stay pretty much at this level for almost a month, but if you really feel good you can move on as suggested at the end of this chapter. In any case, you Competitive Rookies should monitor your bodies carefully during this training period because you are trying to do quite a bit more than ever before. If it proves too difficult, break down the improvement so that it takes a month to accomplish. On the other hand, if you find that it is not too much for you, you are ready to do some real walking in the near future, perhaps even trying your first race.

	Easy Beginner	*Advanced Beginner*	*Competitive Rookie*
Sunday	In form, 1 hr.	In form, 1½ hr.	RW 5 mi. at 12–13 min. pace.
Monday	Rest.	RW 4 mi. at 13–14 min. pace.	RW 6 mi. at 12–13 min. pace.
Tuesday	RW 5 mi. at 14–15 min. pace.	RW 5 mi. at 13–14 min. pace.	RW 4 mi. at 12–13 min. pace.

	Easy Beginner	Advanced Beginner	Competitive Rookie
Wednesday	INT.	INT.	INT.

(By now, you should have moved ten notches ahead on the Improvement Chart, and the faster pace and greater number of repeats should be no more difficult than the first time was.)

	Easy Beginner	Advanced Beginner	Competitive Rookie
Thursday	RW 3 mi. at 13–14 min. pace.	Fartlek, 1½ hr.	Fartlek, 1½ hr.
Friday	Rest.	Rest.	PS in form, 1 hr.
Saturday	RW 3 mi. at 13–14 min. pace.	RW 3 mi. at 12–13 min. pace.	RW 6 mi. at 12–13 min. pace.

The above schedules will give you a feeling of what real walking is all about. The path from those early sixteen-minute miles to the eight-minute ones that a champion can belt out is as uncomplicated as a country road—that is, it will get you there surely if not quite in a straight line or as fast as a super highway. And like the country road, this gradual upgrading of your training will be a pleasant experience.

Although I have created these schedules only to illustrate some of the principles that you will want to follow in building your own individualized training programs, I realize that some of you are going to decide that one of my schedules sounds okay and that you will follow it religiously. That's fine. I still must repeat one bit of advice. You are your own coach. Never forget that. Any time the suggested workout feels much too easy, move up the challenge a bit. But don't increase it too drastically, because once you move up you are supposed to stay at that level, so you are really committing yourself to a series of more challenging workouts every time you increase the number of miles or decrease the number of minutes per mile. Don't put too much pressure on your future workouts.

More likely than finding the work too easy, you will come to a week in which things are tough, when you are really struggling to meet the assigned goals. This is not supposed to happen. ("Train, don't strain," remember?) When you start to strain, simply go back to the week before and repeat that level until you have it under control. Sure, it may take you a month to make two weeks' progress, but as you are taking up walking in terms of a lifetime, how much does it matter whether you reach a certain level on May 17 instead of June 1? Keep thinking in long-range terms, and you will lessen the danger that you will overwork yourself into an aborted walking career.

Competitive Rookies who still do not feel comfortable in planning schedules can be guided by the following rules: Reserve Wednesdays for interval work. The Improvement Chart will tell you what to aim at in months to come. For the fartlek and in-form workouts, keep them in your schedule once a week and build gradually to a two-hour workout in each. That takes care of three of the seven days each week.

For the four racewalking days each week, keep your distances at the ten-week level until you feel comfortable. Then devote one workout a week to a shorter (two- to four-mile) workout at a faster pace. Try to lower your rate by half a minute each month until you reach eleven-minute miles. Then set your improvement goals at fifteen seconds per month.

Your other two workouts should gradually increase the distance, moving up a mile or two each month until you reach twelve miles. That's enough until you get into some races and decide if you want to become a serious racewalker or if the more casual approach that I advocate is sufficient for you.

Once you get serious and start going to races, you'll meet top walkers at races and at clinics, and you will suddenly receive plenty of advice. That advice will be directed at you personally and will be more effective than any advice that a book can give you.

If you want an idea of what a top-level racewalker might have for a schedule, here is a fairly typical one:

Monday: One hour at a pace one minute a mile slower than race pace, interspersed with occasional intervals at race pace, never hard enough to lead to fatigue.

Tuesday: Twelve miles of a hard workout, the pace thirty seconds a mile faster than on Monday, maintained steadily throughout.

Wednesday: One hour of racewalking in form, much like Monday's workout only slower if you are feeling any tiredness from Tuesday.

Thursday: Repeat Tuesday's workout.

Friday: Repeat Wednesday's workout.

Saturday: Twenty-five miles of long, slow distance. The point of this workout is to get your body used to long hours of effort. You can go at just about any pace you choose, but the important thing is to keep on the road for four or five hours.

Sunday: The top effort of the week. It could be a time trial of ten to fifteen miles or a race. (Of course, if the race is an important one, the long, slow distance workout on Saturday would be cut in half or less.)

Alternate Workouts: This schedule will give you about 80 miles a week, over 300 a month, and 4,000 for a year, enough to develop all your potential (and also to use up a considerable percentage of your free time).

If you are this serious about your walking, you will almost certainly incorporate stretching and body building exercises into your program. Such work is always helpful but never necessary. You can achieve world-class form without the exercises, but because the exercises might mean the difference between victory and defeat in a big race, the serious walker will usually add them to his program.

I do not recommend exercises for the average walker, however, because the negative feelings toward exercises are apt to drive out the pleasure of the sport, and for me there is little excuse for taking up racewalking unless you enjoy it.

The other alternate workout the serious walker should consider is interval work. Intervals definitely are a key to fast improvement in walking.

Improvement Chart

9

A *lthough I have emphasized* the fact that you must make
your own coaching decisions, there are certain factors upon
which all sound training is based. In interval work, the way to success
is through gradual improvement, and the following Improvement
Chart will be your guide to safe, sure progress, whether you use it as
the basis for every-other-day workouts or limit yourself to a twice-
a-month check. The basis for the chart is the fact that you are dealing
with three factors in interval work: (1) how fast you go; (2) how many
repetitions you do; and (3) how much you rest between repetitions.

What you must do is find your proper place on the chart and then
work toward improvement from that spot.

Your first step is to find a quarter-mile course. The local high
school track is one easy possibility, or you can measure the distance
accurately on any level surface near your regular training grounds.
(Half-mile and mile courses will work just as well if you have sufficient stamina. Simply double and quadruple the time figures on the
chart.)

Once you have found your quarter mile, go out with a stop watch
or a regular watch with a sweep second hand. Quickly walk a brisk
quarter mile in form, but do not exhaust yourself. Then stroll the
same distance in form but very slowly. Walk a second brisk quarter,

trying to end with the same time as the first. Stroll again, and then walk a third fast quarter. If you are feeling quite tired after three intervals, quit and check your spot on the chart. If you still have energy, do a fourth, fifth, or sixth quarter, stopping only when you are no longer able to equal the time of your first quarter.

Let's say you tired after three intervals. You did the first in three minutes fifty seconds. The second was 3:48, but on the third try you took 3:58. That averages out to 3 × 3:52 on the chart. So you check and find that your next workout should be either 3 × 3:50 or 4 × 4:00. Your improvement may be either down the column (meaning a faster speed) or to the right, meaning that you will go slightly slower but will add another repetition.

If you are doing this several times a week, you should never try to advance more than one step at a time, but if you use the interval chart only once a week or less, you may find that you improve two or three steps at a workout. In such cases, you should move both down the chart (a faster pace) and across the chart (more repetitions).

The difference between one step and the next is imperceptible. Some days you will feel so good that you will want to move ahead several steps all at once. Don't do it. The idea of these workouts is to feel that you could have done more on each one. Then the next time you actually will do more.

If you worked out 100 times a year in this manner (more than I'd recommend for any but the most ardent), you could improve from a 3 × 4:00 turtle to a most respectable 15 × 2:20 workout, one that will leave you ready for a race effort that will beat a good many regular race walkers.

Of course, no one will sail along for a year with uninterrupted progress. The chart is not magic. There will be days when you simply don't improve or when you have to struggle to achieve the next step on the chart. At such times, repeat that particular step on the chart until you feel confident and ready to move up.

Similarly, after you have been ill, say with a cold, you should drop back on the chart to a level that you can manage easily and then build back up from there.

Always remember that train does not mean strain. If you're straining, you are not helping yourself on a daily basis. The all-out efforts should be limited to race days and to time trials, or omitted entirely for those who are not interested in athletic glory but only in the benefits of walking.

STROLL ONE-QUARTER MILE (440 YARDS) BETWEEN INTERVALS

3 ×	4 ×	5 ×	6 ×	7 ×	8 ×	9 ×
4:00	4:00	4:00	4:00	4:00	4:00	4:00
3:58	3:58	3:58	3:58	3:58	3:58	
3:56	3:56	3:56	3:56	3:56	3:56	
3:54	3:54	3:54	3:54	3:54	3:54	
3:52	3:52	3:52	3:52	3:52	3:52	
3:50	3:50	3:50	3:50	3:50		
3:48	3:48	3:48	3:48	3:48		
3:46	3:46	3:46	3:46	3:46		
3:44	3:44	3:44	3:44	3:44		
3:42	3:42	3:42	3:42			
3:40	3:40	3:40	3:40			
3:38	3:38	3:38	3:38			
3:36	3:36	3:36	3:36			
3:34	3:34	3:34				
3:32	3:32	3:32				
3:30	3:30	3:30				
3:28	3:28	3:28				
3:26	3:26					
3:24	3:24					
3:22	3:22					
3:20	3:20					
3:18						
3:16						
3:14						
3:12						

STROLL ONE-QUARTER MILE (440 YARDS)
BETWEEN INTERVALS

3 ×	4 ×	5 ×	6 ×	7 ×	8 ×	9 ×
3:10	3:18	3:26	3:34	3:42	3:50	3:58
3:08	3:16	3:24	3:32	3:40	3:48	3:56
3:06	3:14	3:22	3:30	3:38	3:46	3:54
3:04	3:12	3:20	3:28	3:36	3:44	3:52
3:02	3:10	3:18	3:26	3:34	3:42	3:50
3:00	3:08	3:16	3:24	3:32	3:40	3:48
2:58	3:06	3:14	3:22	3:30	3:38	3:46
2:56	3:04	3:12	3:20	3:28	3:36	3:44
2:54	3:02	3:10	3:18	3:26	3:34	3:42
2:52	3:00	3:08	3:16	3:24	3:32	3:40
2:50	2:58	3:06	3:14	3:22	3:30	3:38
2:48	2:56	3:04	3:12	3:20	3:28	3:36
2:46	2:54	3:02	3:10	3:18	3:26	3:34
2:44	2:52	3:00	3:08	3:16	3:24	3:32
2:42	2:50	2:58	3:06	3:14	3:22	3:30
2:40	2:48	2:56	3:04	3:12	3:20	3:28
2:38	2:46	2:54	3:02	3:10	3:18	3:26
2:36	2:44	2:52	3:00	3:08	3:16	3:24
2:34	2:42	2:50	2:58	3:06	3:14	3:22
2:32	2:40	2:48	2:56	3:04	3:12	3:20
2:30	2:38	2:46	2:54	3:02	3:10	3:18
	2:36	2:44	2:52	3:00	3:08	3:16
	2:34	2:42	2:50	2:58	3:06	3:14
	2:32	2:40	2:48	2:56	3:04	3:12

STROLL ONE-QUARTER MILE (440 YARDS) BETWEEN INTERVALS

4 × 2:30	5 ×	6 ×	7 ×	8 ×	9 ×	10 ×
						3:16
						3:14
						3:12
					3:10	3:10
					3:08	3:08
					3:06	3:06
					3:04	3:04
				3:02	3:02	3:02
				3:00	3:00	3:00
				2:58	2:58	2:58
				2:56	2:56	2:56
			2:54	2:54	2:54	2:54
			2:52	2:52	2:52	2:52
			2:50	2:50	2:50	2:50
			2:48	2:48	2:48	2:48
		2:46	2:46	2:46	2:46	2:46
		2:44	2:44	2:44	2:44	2:44
		2:42	2:42	2:42	2:42	2:42
		2:40	2:40	2:40	2:40	2:40
	2:38	2:38	2:38	2:38	2:38	2:38
	2:36	2:36	2:36	2:36	2:36	2:36
	2:34	2:34	2:34	2:34	2:34	2:34
	2:32	2:32	2:32	2:32	2:32	2:32
2:30	2:30	2:30	2:30	2:30	2:30	2:30

STROLL 220 YARDS
BETWEEN INTERVALS

9 ×	10 ×	11 ×	12 ×	13 ×	14 ×	15 ×
2:56	3:00	3:00	3:00	3:00	3:00	3:00
2:54	2:58	2:58	2:58	2:58	2:58	2:58
2:52	2:56	2:56	2:56	2:56	2:56	2:56
2:50	2:54	2:54	2:54	2:54	2:54	2:54
2:48	2:52	2:52	2:52	2:52	2:52	2:52
2:46	2:50	2:50	2:50	2:50	2:50	2:50
2:44	2:48	2:48	2:48	2:48	2:48	2:48
2:42	2:46	2:46	2:46	2:46	2:46	2:46
2:40	2:44	2:44	2:44	2:44	2:44	2:44
2:38	2:42	2:42	2:42	2:42	2:42	2:42
2:36	2:40	2:40	2:40	2:40	2:40	2:40
2:34	2:38	2:38	2:38	2:38	2:38	2:38
2:32	2:36	2:36	2:36	2:36	2:36	2:36
2:30	2:34	2:34	2:34	2:34	2:34	2:34
2:29	2:32	2:32	2:32	2:32	2:32	2:32
2:28	2:30	2:30	2:30	2:30	2:30	
2:27	2:29	2:29	2:29	2:29	2:29	
2:26	2:28	2:28	2:28	2:28		
2:25	2:27	2:27	2:27	2:27		
2:24	2:26	2:26	2:26			
2:23	2:25	2:25	2:25			
2:22	2:24	2:24				
2:21	2:23	2:23				
2:20	2:22					
2:18	2:21					

STROLL 220 YARDS BETWEEN INTERVALS

9 ×	10 ×	11 ×	12 ×	13 ×	14 ×	15 ×
2:18	2:20	2:22	2:24	2:26	2:28	2:30
2:17	2:19	2:21	2:23	2:25	2:27	2:29
2:16	2:18	2:20	2:22	2:24	2:26	2:28
2:15	2:17	2:19	2:21	2:23	2:25	2:27
2:14	2:16	2:18	2:20	2:22	2:24	2:26
2:13	2:15	2:17	2:19	2:21	2:23	2:25
2:12	2:14	2:16	2:18	2:20	2:22	2:24
2:11	2:13	2:15	2:17	2:19	2:21	2:23
2:10	2:12	2:14	2:16	2:18	2:20	2:22
2:09	2:11	2:13	2:15	2:17	2:19	2:21
2:08	2:10	2:12	2:14	2:16	2:18	2:20
2:07	2:09	2:11	2:13	2:15	2:17	2:19
2:06	2:08	2:10	2:12	2:14	2:16	2:18
2:05	2:07	2:09	2:11	2:13	2:15	2:17
2:04	2:06	2:08	2:10	2:12	2:14	2:16
2:03	2:05	2:07	2:09	2:11	2:13	2:15
2:02	2:04	2:06	2:08	2:10	2:12	2:14
2:01	2:03	2:05	2:07	2:09	2:11	2:13
2:00	2:02	2:04	2:06	2:08	2:10	2:12
1:59	2:01	2:03	2:05	2:07	2:09	2:11
1:58	2:00	2:02	2:04	2:06	2:08	2:10
1:57	1:59	2:01	2:03	2:05	2:07	2:09
1:56	1:58	2:00	2:02	2:04	2:06	2:08
	1:57	1:59	2:01	2:03	2:05	2:07
	1:56	1:58	2:00	2:02	2:04	2:06

10

How Can You Gain Extra Upper-Body Strength?

*A*lthough *racewalking exercises the* whole body and develops upper body strength without any supplementary work, there is no denying that any collection of serious racewalkers includes many more Woody Allen types than Burt Reynolds look-alikes. These scrawny guys have huge reservoirs of surprising strength, but most of them could use extra muscles if they were to switch to tennis, golf, softball, or any other sport that calls for powerful arm work.

If you are among those who feel a need for stronger arms, consider increasing your upper body strength by walking with light weights in each hand. It's quite different from the gym work of Olympic weight lifters or body builders as you can quickly tell from the fact that the weights you'll be working with vary mostly from one to five pounds.

For many racewalkers, the weights will prove unnecessary, but everyone should at least consider the benefits and add weight walking to the weekly program if it seems to have possibilities for the individual.

If we divide the readers of this book into three general groups, we will find that only one of the three really will need to get into this weight work. The first group consists of those who take up racewalking somewhat seriously to get to be fast enough to enter local races. The second group is made up of those who merely want to get into reasonably good shape and to be able to eat what they want without getting fat; these walkers are not really interested in competition. The third group represents those who are serious about a sport but not racewalking; these people use the training as a backup to their main sport.

The first group—the ones who want to race—really don't need the weight work. They are going to get very strong anyway, and they won't profit from extra muscles in the upper body.

Members of the second group can also do without the weight work because they will find that racewalking gives them everything they are looking for in the way of health and good feelings about themselves.

That leaves only the third group to take up weight walking. Of course, perhaps many of you will turn out to be like me, namely one who wants to race with some success but also to play another sport as well. For me, that means that if I want to get stronger in the arms and boost performance at tennis and golf, I can profit from walking with weights. I came to this conclusion comparatively recently after forty years of running and walking without the extra exercise, but I'm already convinced that weight walking is effective. I do it moderately, putting my regular racewalk training ahead of the boost-my-tennis weight work, but I still find time for at least a brief weight session perhaps once a week. This is probably below the minimum of weight work if one expects to gain anything from it.

Women and Weight Work

For women, there is a special consideration. Lack of upper-body strength is their most common physical weakness compared to men. Any way for women to develop arm and shoulder strength is worth investigating, especially a way that gives strength without producing the bulging muscles of a weight lifter.

"Heavyhands"

Thus, many racewalkers should be aware of an exercise system christened "Heavyhands" by its inventor, Dr. Leonard Schwartz. In 1982, Dr. Schwartz wrote a book also entitled *Heavyhands*, and in it he gives 278 pages of detailed information about his discovery.

Dr. Schwartz gives so many details of scientific proof of his method's success that I'm sure he's accurate. I'm also sure that I could never discipline myself to do a sufficient percentage of the more than fifty Heavyhands exercises and variants that he suggests, a great majority of them done indoors.

On the other hand, I know from personal experience that weight work is effective. That's because I made a similar discovery of my own many years ago. Besides my walking and running, I always played tennis, and for thirteen years I had my own court and became fairly successful in local competition. Although I could keep playing almost indefinitely as far as my legs were concerned, I lacked both strength and stamina in the arms. (At that time, I was running in practice much more than I racewalked.)

Then I realized that walking was a better sport for me, both because I had more proficiency at it and because it was so safe, so I started to include a large percentage of heel-and-toe time in my workouts. At the same time, I started swinging weights indoors each morning and evening. I have a low threshold of boredom for such things, but I found I was able to take ten imitation forehand swings, ten backhand swings, and ten serves with each hand, sixty swings in all, with a five-pound weight in each hand. That took me less than three minutes per session, and I managed to do it quite faithfully for a period of years.

Without taking scientific measurements at any time except for weighing myself, I still was convinced that the three minutes did improve my strength for tennis. There is no way to tell how much came from swinging the weights and how much came from the benefits of my increased racewalking training, but I definitely became stronger in tennis and my arms developed some of the stamina that my legs had always had.

One way to judge my increased upper-body strength is according to my weight. I first did the exercises about fifteen years ago, and in those days if I trained very hard my weight would go down to around 137 pounds. During this past year I have put in more miles of training and racing than ever before (about 2,400 miles), and I'm in good shape. My weight is right at 144, and I'm sure there is no way short of serious illness that I could get it lower than 141 or 142. I like to think that the extra pounds represent increased upper-body muscle and that I am stronger than ever before in my life.

One thing that keeps me from trying a true Heavyhands schedule is the fact that most of the exercises are done indoors. They are calisthenics, and I've already shared with you my feelings about calisthenics. I avoid them, and I suggest that anyone who wants to keep the fun in exercise should do the same. I feel that my forty-plus years of walking and running attest to the fact that I have found out how to enjoy myself, and one of the key things in this enjoyment is to walk outside where there are interesting things to look at. Everywhere I've ever lived has had such interesting spots, whether it's my present beautiful Cape Cod or undeniably ugly Tokyo. The inside of my house simply is not fascinating enough.

Thus, with one exception all my weight work is done while I'm out walking. However, the outdoors brings another problem. Although I have built up an immunity to ridicule over the years and can now racewalk anywhere, I still don't feel ready to go public with my swinging-arms walking with weights. Therefore, I do my weight walking in the dark, either before my neighbors are awake in the morning or after they are firmly fastened to their television sets at night. If I come across someone while I'm doing weight walking, I just stop swinging and stroll along carrying the weights at my side until the car or pedestrian has passed.

If I were to live in a more crowded area, I'd do my weight walking on the local track or in a lonely park. I'm making a point of my own fear of looking foolish so that those who feel the same will at least know that they have company. The ideal thing would be to have one or more partners out there with you because if misery loves company, exhibitionists love it even more. I'll do crazy things as long as I have someone to do them with me.

Setting Up a Schedule

All weight-work schedules must be tailored to the individual—meaning, as with your regular walking schedule, that you must make the decisions for yourself. There is no one way that is best for all; therefore, until you find a full-time coach, you must make the decisions alone.

I can tell you some of the things you do not need for weight walking, however, and one of these is devoting huge chunks of time for weight work only. All you need to do is take the weights with you on your regular workout. You will be starting with one or two pounds in each hand, so it isn't going to be very bulky. In addition, if you train in lonely terrain, you can do the weight walking for the number of minutes you have decided on and then hide the weights to be picked up on the way back when you'll complete the second half of your weight walking for the day.

If you work out on a track, there's no problem. You can lay the weights down at any time. In the city or thickly settled town where you wouldn't dare try to hide the weights, you can go around the block or several blocks and drop the weights off at your own house, or you could go past a friend's house and do the same.

Equipment

In any case, my point is that you can take a few minutes for weight walking at the start and end of your regular training session. It won't change the regular workout very much, although your arms will feel more tired than usual, of course.

Another thing you won't need is leg weights or weighted belts. Although there are weight programs that advise walking with ankle weights or weights strapped around your middle, I have tried this method and have talked to other walkers who have tried it, and none of us feels that such weights or belts are worthwhile. The ankle weights, for example, slow down your leg speed, and because quickness is one of the two keys to racewalking success, the ankle weights are working against that goal. As for weighted belts around the waist, they make you heavier and make your legs work harder, but they are uncomfortable and somewhat superfluous as your middle is already getting a superb workout. Compared to the versatility of hand weights, the other types of weights are too limited to bother with.

A third thing you don't have to do is purchase expensive equipment. I'd suggest that you start with anything you can find. Walk with a light weight from a lifting set, with a convenient shape like a hammer or a bag of sand, or anything else that gives you a pound or two for each hand. If the workouts please you, you can go out and buy equipment, but I always hate to see people buy things and then decide they aren't going to need them after all. If you do invest in expensive weight equipment and then don't use it, there's going to be a little adverse psychological dig at your confidence every time you look at the things and a small, secret voice says, "See! You just don't have it as an athlete. No guts, no determination." Hammers and bags of sand won't talk to you like that.

If you get hooked on the idea of weight walking, you'll have a choice of things to buy. It's all so new right now that you should check with your local sporting goods store for advice before you decide what to purchase. I suggest that you construct your own weights.

Getting Started

Whatever you decide to use for weights, start gradually. There's no rush about anything when you're working on a lifetime basis. I started with 2½-pound weights from an old set we've had down in the cellar for ages. The pieces were round and smooth with a nice hole in the center for my thumbs. I found that I could handle that weight fairly easily, although I did tire quite fast. But remember that I'd been swinging five-pound weights tennis-style for many years, so I was somewhat used to the system. Don't feel that you're showing a lack of courage if you start with one pound or less in each hand. Believe me, even one pound will start to feel heavy enough when you do some of the more vigorous exercises.

I wouldn't use weights for more than ten minutes on the first day. Then I would see how much stiffness there was the next day and add (or subtract) minutes accordingly. As long as you don't do anything foolish, you'll find that working with weights as you walk along is as safe as racewalking itself.

I suggest that you try all of my ideas and select the ones that seem to work for you. "Work" does not mean that you immediately grow stronger but merely that you enjoy the feeling and are not bored or otherwise turned off by the exercise. Remember that "If you don't like it, drop it" is a good motto.

The exercise I would suggest that you try on your first time out is the obvious one. Take your weights and walk in normal racewalking style. You won't bring your arm quite as high on the backswing, and you will want to go a bit higher on the forward swing, but in general you will walk quite normally, especially if you don't try to carry too heavy a weight the first time.

One of the first things to watch out for is to make sure you don't hit your hip with the weight as your arm swings through on each stride. Even a one-pound weight can hurt, and if you get as high as five pounds, you can give yourself quite a nasty bruise if you're careless. Women with their wider hips must be extra careful. Fortunately, the natural hip action can be coordinated with the arm action in such a way as to give extra space for protection against touching the hips. I say "touching" because even if you only brush your hip on the swing through, the repeated effects of such light touches of metal on flesh can add up to a painful bruise.

Anyway, your first weight-walking attempt should find you carrying light weights and using the normal racewalking style of arm action. I have suggested a maximum of ten minutes at a time, repeated no more than once, for the first few days.

The other exercises that I have developed for myself are all aimed at special goals such as strengthening my back, developing the muscles for tennis and golf, and improving upper body strength. In deciding which exercises to use, I follow my basic philosophy of keeping what feels good and dropping what feels bad. No doubt a coach could drive me to work more efficiently and to persevere through unpleasant workouts, but I stay loyal to my EEO ways (Enjoyable Exercise Only).

Try some of the things that have worked for me, and add your own inventions. I believe that you will develop a more satisfactory personal exercise program than any general-type strategy can offer. Your program will be specifically for you; the general programs supposedly work for all the world.

Back Problems

One thing that a large percentage of the world shares with me is a well-founded worry about back problems. I have found weight walking to be a real help in strengthening my back, and I have had none of my recurring miseries since I started doing back exercises. What I do is walk bent over forward at the waist. I look as though I'm suffering from a terrible stitch in my side, but, of course, all I'm doing is forcing my back muscles to support the weight of my upper body.

It's no great strain, at least not the way I do it. I walk along bent over with my arms dangling at my side, carrying my 2½ pounds in each hand. After I get used to doing that, I add a shortened version of the racewalker's arm swing to my bent-over walk. Eventually, I can bring the arms higher than my back on the rear swing and about head high on the forward swing.

As with everything involved in developing increasingly tough workouts, this back exercise involves three factors: how long I do it, how heavy the weights are, and how much effort I'm putting into the swing. I can go along at a slow pace with little arm action for a long way, or I can go at near maximum pace for short, repeated intervals.

Now in my sixties, I must be more careful than younger walkers. My own way is to do it all in moderation. I have never pushed myself through an all-out maximum effort weight-walking session. I keep track of the number of minutes at each level of exertion, and I make sure that the early workouts of any new exercise are done so painlessly that the next time I have no trouble increasing the first output. I'm sure that I could push myself harder and develop faster, but I prefer to err on the side of safety.

A third back-building exercise in my weight-walking repertoire consists of long straight-arm swings with both arms going forward and backward at the same time as though I were a badly bent pendulum. At first, I keep the swings fairly short to get the feel of it and to make sure I'm not going to hit a hip, but as I get into the rhythm of the double-arm swing, I increase the exertion and I find it gets my pulse going.

This double-arm swing can also be used with an erect racewalking form, again with both arms straightened out, not bent. A variant is to grasp the weights together with both hands in front of me and then swing the weights from side to side as I walk. This exercise is good for shoulder development. This is one time when you should not attempt to place your feet in an exact straight line with each other. A wider-apart walking style will give you better balance as the weights go from your left to right to left. As a general rule, you should not think about your racewalking form when you're doing weight walking. There will be a large percentage of your training time when you walk with no weights, and that is the time for style work.

The next exercises that I suggest for a weight-walking program are those related to a sport in which you hope to add strength. It makes simple good sense that if you use your muscles in weight walking in the same movement pattern that you use in your sport, you'll be strengthening yourself for your specialty as you do the odd-looking weight work. For me, this means carrying an imaginary tennis racket in each hand and swinging forehand and backhand as I walk along. It's important to do the same exercises with each hand because tennis players and others tend to develop their strength in a one-sided way, and anything like weight walking that balances the development is going to be beneficial. I also serve as I walk along.

The pattern that I have developed is to take four walking strides and then use a two-stride cycle to make my imitation strokes, turning to the side slightly as I do so. I do my ten right-hand forehands in a row, then the ten left-handed ones. I have tried alternating left- and right-hand swings, but I seem to lack the coordination to handle it smoothly. The whole thing takes fewer than 400 strides—about three minutes in all. At first, I had trouble coordinating the swings and the walk, and I had to do it very deliberately before I could pick up the rhythm, but now I can go as fast and swing as hard as I want.

I also have an awkward golf swing imitation that I use with both hands on the same weight. I turn my body somewhat to the side, taking my normal swing, then doing approximately the same as though I were a left-handed golfer. I take around ten strides between each two swings because it is quite awkward and because I haven't worked hard enough at this particular swing to have much smoothness.

A few times in the past I have tried to relieve my old hockey glory. I never did have the strength for a powerful shot, and I wish I had had the weight-swing method to help me. Now I occasionally walk with my two hands together in front of me in a pattern similar to the side-to-side exercise for strengthening the back. As I go from left to right, I pretend I'm stickhandling the puck the length of the ice, and when I approach the goal I raise my weights and come down with a big slap shot. Although I haven't skated for years, I'd bet that I have a better shot now than I ever did in my high school days.

As you coach yourself through your early weight-walking workouts, keep these possibilities in mind: You may find these are the kinds of exercise you really enjoy. You wish you could do more and more.

A second possibility will be that you agree with me that while weight work is less enjoyable than regular racewalking, it's only a minor annoyance. The fact that you can develop your upper body beyond the limits of racewalking will be enough for you to incorporate the weight work into your schedule a minimum of three times a week. (Remember that that doesn't mean you do nothing but weight walking three times a week, just that you do it as part of the workout those three times.)

The third and most likely possibility is that you're not going to want to do weight work at all. You are getting all the benefits you need from racewalking alone, and weight walking turns an enjoyable outing into a work session that you find yourself starting to dread. So you don't add it to your program, and you won't be missing anything vital.

An Indoor Workout

There is one addition to weight walking that everyone will want to consider, and it may tip the scales in favor of the exercise in some instances. Perhaps the biggest advantage for me in weight walking is that I can avoid bad weather and still get in a workout. Not only do I get the exercise, but I do it with less boredom than I usually find in calisthenics.

What I do is walk in place from the start to the end of a thirty-minute television program. As all racewalking, including walking in place, demands that your head be kept still, I can exercise vigorously and still focus easily on the screen. It certainly lessens the boredom of indoor exercise to be able to watch television, and the thirty-minute workout can be made as aerobic as you want. You must discipline yourself to lift your feet at least two-thirds of the height of the other knee, a foot or so off the ground for one of average height.

The information about pulse rate in Chapter 5 will show you how beneficial weight walking can be. Your pulse rate will definitely move up to the 75% maximum range that you are looking for, and you will know that with weight walking much of the energy expended (and hence much of the benefit) will be in the upper body.

A minimum rate of 120 steps per minute will give you a workout and is simple to check on because it means two steps every second, and a glance at the second hand of a clock or watch will tell you whether you are maintaining that pace. I suggest intervals of faster work, perhaps during commercials, although at first you will want to maintain a steady pace throughout to make sure you finish the thirty minutes.

These indoor sessions will exercise the upper body more than the legs, and, of course, they do little good for your racewalking style. However, compared to walking outdoors in a winter rain or a blizzard, they are quite satisfactory.

There are also variations on the arm action that you can use as you walk in place. There is the normal walking pattern in which the right arm goes back as the right leg goes forward. Second, there is the suggestion for outdoor walking in which both arms go forward and back together, and finally, although I have trouble with the coordination, you can swing your right arm forward as the right leg goes forward so your body turns first left and then right as you walk in place. This third method effectively avoids bumping yourself with the weights.

In planning your weight work, you must decide how important upper-body strength is to your athletic future. If you merely want to stay in shape, lose weight, and feel good about your body, the weight work isn't necessary. If you do take it up, light weights (one or two pounds in each hand) are all you will ever need. Probably weighted gloves will be the most convenient for you as they will keep you warm in cool weather, can be worn under heavy wool mittens in cold weather, and will free you from worry about banging your hips because the weights will be on the backs of your hands, away from the body.

If you are as economy minded as I am and you don't want to go beyond a couple of pounds of weight for your work, you'll be able to figure out a homemade weight that will suit your personal needs.

In summary, if you never try weight walking at all, you'll be perfectly all right and your upper body will gain strength just through the normal style of racewalking. If you want a maximum-benefit weight-walking program, you can keep adding your own ideas to the exercises I have suggested. A full racewalking schedule supplemented by a well-developed weight program will soon have you well on your way to owning a super body that will come as close as possible to a maximum utilization of your potential.

You will have health and strength that you never knew before. You can't lose. Make an honest estimate of your own determination and self-discipline, balance that against your personal goals as an athlete, and then set up your own program. As long as you are honest with yourself, you should find that you are able to keep to your plans and enjoy the exercise.

Never forget the enjoyment factor. It's much better to embark on a minimum-effort, enjoyable exercise program that lasts a lifetime than to force yourself to do marvelous things for six months, after which you go back to beer bloat and body bulge because you couldn't endure the hard work any longer.

11

Where Should You Do Your Walking?

A t first, telling you where to take your training walks may sound like the most unnecessary advice possible. Of course, you're going to pick out a convenient, safe, attractive area and train there. It's so obvious.

Although I have a definite bias in favor of walkers as opposed to runners, I don't really think there's a great difference between the two species. You must have noticed, as I have, that runners have practically no common sense when it comes to selecting places to run.

I live on Cape Cod, one of the most attractive places on the East Coast, and yet when I drive down Route 28, which is ugly, commercialized, and crowded, I see runners everywhere; but when I go to the beautiful side roads, the firmly packed sand on the deserted beaches, and the power lines, parks, and other out-of-the-way areas, I almost always am by myself.

Furthermore, when my friends find a good course to cover, they seem to run only on that particular course, time after time, year after year.

So my advice to you is to vary your courses. There is something spiritual to any human activity and especially to a purely natural act like walking, even more so to walking out in nature. If you want to develop a lifetime habit of walking, it is certainly going to help if you can find beautiful surroundings for your walks.

Of course, the most obvious courses for you to follow are those that start and end at your home. You go out the front door and turn right or left, and you have your two chief routes lying before you. That should be your bread-and-butter route, the one you take when you are pressed for time.

You can hardly find a spot in the entire United States, however, where a ten-minute drive or less won't take you to a different type of area from the one in which you live. Although I am hardly a worldly traveler, I have lived at one time or another in a couple of Boston suburbs; in Stillwater, Oklahoma; Boulder, Colorado; New Haven, Connecticut; Canton, Mississippi; Ann Arbor, Michigan; Spruce Point, Maine; Brewster, Massachusetts; and Tokyo, Japan. That's pretty good variety, and in all of these places I have found beautiful and fascinating places to do my training.

Tokyo is hardly a contender for the world's loveliest city title, but I found great places to walk there. The same holds true for each of the other places, all of them with more natural beauty than Tokyo.

If you are in a city, parks are one key as to where to walk. In a town, it may take only a short drive away from the center to bring you to a lovely country setting. It's definitely worth the short drive and the wasted gasoline to give yourself a break from your regular routine.

I also recommend finding places where your dogs can run with you. For me, this means going to the town dump and walking from there along the power lines that pass nearby. We have a leash law in our town that puts my three old dogs in the law-breakers' role whenever they trot down a residential street, but no one minds them behind the dump or along the nice flat dirt road that winds along the power lines.

Another thing that is good about walking in different places is that it takes the pressure off you a bit and enables you to relax more on a training day that is supposed to be an easy one. If you are covering your regular course, you know exactly where each mile is, and as you glance at your watch, you're suddenly aware of just what your pace is, and you may find yourself pushing the pace a bit more than you meant to. On the other hand, when you are walking over unmeasured roads and paths, you have only one guide to follow—

your watch—and the time keeps ticking away toward your goal of an hour or so. It doesn't matter how fast you go, time will move at the same pace. That's what I mean by keeping pressure off yourself and keeping an easy workout just as easy as you had planned on its being.

As in all else, I believe that I would be hurting instead of helping you if I set up hard-and-fast rules as to where you should train. But for those who like specific examples, I can say that I train over a measured course right from my own house about five times out of ten. Another two of the ten are free and easy outings along the power lines or on the beach. One more is going out with a friend or with my daughter on a course that's regular for my partner but only a once-in-a-while place for me. The other two times I try to divide between an interval outing on the track and a walk either over an area that I have never trod before or one that I haven't been to for a long time.

I like variety, and I know it's good for me. After all, I am using the workouts to prepare for races, and the races are in lots of different places. Therefore, it only makes sense to get variety into my training sites as well.

Probably the more poetic you are, the more important it is for you to find varying and fascinating places to train. The all-business types perhaps can thrive equally well on repeated laps around the neighborhood, the same course every day, the only variety being the number of laps for the day and the speed at which each lap is covered.

I once knew a guy who charted every workout he took and took every workout on the same course, plotting its speed and distance against the speed and distance of that day the year before (and the month before and the week before). He could show curves that represented his success for each of those weeks, months, and years. He loved his records, and they were as much an incentive for him as my beautiful courses are for me.

One thing that I recommend for all racewalkers, whether they're poetic or scientific, is to tailor their courses to any upcoming race they may be entered in. Cape Cod, for example, is not big on mountains, but if I'm going into a race that has its own Heartbreak Hill, I try to do as much hill work as possible. I don't have any trouble finding hills on Cape Cod. I have the road up to the fire tower in Nickerson State Park in Brewster or the Shore Road stretch between Lighthouse and Coast Guard beaches in Eastham, or the roller coaster access roads along the hillier stretches of Route 6, the Mid Cape Highway. If I can find plenty of hills on Cape Cod, almost any area will have hills for you to train on.

Similarly, if you are worried about the possibility of heat on the day of a race, do your training in the open sun at noon. Also do it on a track or other area where copious water will be available. Remember how important water is to survival in heat. I once finished a race—a running race, I'm happy to say, not walking—behind a young man who missed the turn into the parking lot for the final 200 yards. I was unsporting enough to let the guy go the wrong way, and I darted around the corner and beat him to the finish. Then I turned around and walked back to my daughter Linda who was coming along behind me in the race, and when I reached the little turn that the young man had missed, they were putting him into the emergency rescue vehicle. It was a very quick rescue; it couldn't have been even five minutes after he had taken the little wrong turn and then evidently had turned around and collapsed, but in spite of the swift rescue attempt, the young man died that night at Cape Cod Hospital, the only fatality I've ever known in a race I entered. Because his job was such that he'd always trained in the evening, and some misguided old-timer had told him that taking water slowed you down too much, his lack of heat training proved fatal. Heat affects runners and walkers alike. It's sheer folly to fool around with heat, so do your training for a potentially hot race by finding a hot place to train.

Another feature of a training course that I recommend is having mileage markers. In Massachusetts, there are tenth-of-a-mile markers on all state highways, and even though they are somewhat casually placed, the average is accurate as are the bigger mile markers. I try to incorporate a mile or two of highway on some of my courses, just to get in the measured distances to check my pace.

I also have discovered how many steps I take to a quarter mile. It's a simple process: Just go to the local high school track and walk around and around, counting your steps for a lap (or a half lap) at various times in your workout. You'll find that you take slightly fewer strides per quarter mile when you're fresh compared to when you're tired, but basically you'll find that your average total comes out almost the same on every lap.

Once you know that it takes you, say, 454 strides to go around a quarter-mile track, you can go to your own unmarked course and lay out quarter miles every time you have taken 454 strides. I've said before that you shouldn't put pressure on yourself and time every single workout, but if you lay out quarter miles (a spot of paint on the road or on a tree or post is all you need to remind you of where the quarter miles occur) on your own favorite course, you'll have a training route on which you can do quarter- or half-mile intervals any time you choose.

I also like to have the final mile or half mile of a regular training course marked out, and then sometimes when I'm feeling good at the end of an easy training walk, I can pick it up for the final stretch and finish with a fast half mile or mile. It's good for the morale to know you've walked fast and to have proof in the form of time on a measured course (as opposed to *thinking* you probably were moving fast but not being quite sure).

Incidentally, when you measure your courses, be sure to do so by the so-many-steps-per-lap method I've suggested. Car odometers are notoriously inaccurate. For example, on the two cars in our family right now, one measures a mile as 0.95 miles while the other calls it 1.05. Those 1/20 of a mile increments can lead you into seriously misjudging what you're doing as far as speed is concerned because 1/20 of a mile takes even a good racewalker close to thirty seconds to cover. With the counting-steps system, your margin of error will be more like one-in-fifty, usually less.

If you're already hard-pressed for time in your day's schedule, you may feel that getting out the car and driving to a place to walk is simply too wasteful when you could just step out your front door and start to walk with no preliminaries. But when you consider that even at thirty miles an hour you can go five miles in ten minutes, and when you further consider that maintaining the enjoyable side of walking is the key to doing it day after day, year after year, the ten minutes of driving that can make your workout a beautiful part of your day seems like a good investment.

My real message in this chapter is to encourage you to think about where you're going to do your walking and to be sure your goals include the aesthetic as well as the athletic. If lovely sites become an integral part of your training plans, you're several steps further along the road to a successful career, remembering always that success involves the pleasure principle as well as the practical.

12

Do You Have to Give Up Other Sports to Walk?

Although I have been advocating walking as a great sport, one worth all the time you can spend on it and one worth traveling miles and miles to compete in, there is no question that racewalking also is ideal as a backup sport to almost any other activity you take seriously. You don't have to become a fanatic to profit from racewalking.

For example, sports like golf and bowling demand tremendous skill but can hardly be said to get you into top physical condition. A daily or every-other-day walk can be coordinated with any less active sport and keep you in top condition with a minimum of time expended.

Walking also goes well with more active sports like tennis and the other racket sports, softball, swimming, and the strenuous team sports. Unless you live in the South on the beach or have unlimited access to a pool, you can hardly swim whenever you want. You can always walk. You can't play team sports unless you have a team there with you. You can always walk. Tennis is no good in the rain and it's too expensive to play indoors every day. Walking every day costs you only a new pair of shoes once in a long, long while. Bowling, curling, golf, and just about any sport you can name all either involve getting together at a special place with special equipment and the right partners, are very expensive, or are dependent on the weather or another variable. Only walking and running are possible at all times in all places in spite of what the weather may be. And we hope we've already convinced you that for a large majority of the population walking makes more sense than running.

Walking for Runners

Even for the runner, walking makes a fine second sport. Of course, if you are a champion-level runner, walking may be something that you won't want to risk. I suppose the muscles are used somewhat differently and that a Bill Rodgers might slow down a couple of seconds per mile if he did part of his training in walking style. I really don't know. I don't need to know, however, because the advice in this book is for those athletes who take their sports a little more casually than a Rodgers, a Chris Evert-Lloyd, or a Reggie Jackson. I do know that I've run some of my best races after training exclusively by walking for weeks before.

What do you get if you decide to combine walking with your present sport? And how do you go about making this combination work most effectively for you?

First, you get overall conditioning. Take tennis, for example. Now, tennis can be one of the most demanding of sports. A four-hour singles match demands stamina more akin to the marathon or a forty-kilometer walk than most things in sports. The thing about four-hour singles matches is that you never know when one is going to come along. Two players can face each other and the games can go quickly. Then player A can break serve in the first set and win, 6–4. The two even players again have only one service break in the second set. Player A gets that one also and wins 6–3. They play nineteen games with few long deuce games. Everything is over in less than an hour.

Then, in the next tournament, A and B meet again, and this time the scores go 7–6, 6–7, 7–5, or something like that. That's exactly twice as many games they played as the first time they met, and this time the games went on longer and longer as the two grew too tired to hit so many winners and were too determined to hit any losers. The match can thus stretch to three or four hours.

My rather wordy point here is that you have no idea as to when you are going to be put into a marathon-type situation in tennis. The situation doesn't arise regularly and you can't train for it. But if you are a walker on the side, you can develop as much stamina as you feel you need, and as you build it, you also will be building strength in your arms and body, strength that will translate into stronger basic strokes in tennis.

Recently in a local Cape Cod tournament, the same player had to play three straight three-set matches on the final day. Most people felt that Greg would be the weak link in the third of these doubles matches because the other three players had had only two matches that day, but I knew that Greg was putting in six miles a day besides his tennis, and I felt that fatigue would be a minor factor for him. Sure enough, he won his last serve of the match and then was the dominant player in the final tie breaker, all of this due in part at least to the miles that Greg had put in on the roads. (That he did it running, not walking, doesn't spoil the lesson that I'm trying to put across here.)

Because of the nervous strain in any big contest, in bowling, golf (even when you ride in a cart), or anything else, a player gets tired and fatigue becomes a factor. Thus, in less active sports such as pool and billiards, for example, although the Minnesota Fats types are going to do very well, the normal person will do slightly better if he is in top shape than if he has a roll of fat around his middle.

The real benefit of racewalking for the devotees of non-stamina sports is the overall conditioning that racewalking gives you that your own sport can't offer.

And racewalking gives it so easily, at so small an expense of time with so little risk of injury. If you can spare three hours a week—either three one-hour sessions or six half-hour ones—you can improve your own conditioning perceptibly. In time, you may even get back the investment when you reach the end of your life; that is, you may live a few years longer due to those three hours of walking each week.

More certain and much more immediate, you will get rewards in the form of better appetite and better conscience when you do eat well, and better sleep for the simple reason that you will need better sleep.

You will also save time and money because you won't have to join the local fitness club, you won't have to buy books on dieting, and you won't have to watch Richard Simmons on TV as you try to do all the "enjoyable" exercises he ingeniously devises for you.

Of course, I realize that not all people are as reluctant to do exercises as I am. Some people love them, I guess. If you do, keep on. Fitness center activities go very well with walking. You can even do your walking by heel and toeing it to and from the place of exercise if it's a convenient distance from your home.

I can summarize and end this chapter by saying that because racewalking exercises the whole body and does it in such a way that you can take a good workout without exhausting yourself, racewalking becomes an ideal companion sport for just about any other sport that you can name.

My friend John Ottow has a common-sense summary of the advantages of walking. John's chronic back problem forced him to give up running, and he has switched to walking and loves it. He says, "Walking has a tremendous range of motion. It brings all the muscles into play, and thus you don't tighten up so much. Everything works in a balanced way."

Walking doesn't upset the balance of your life either. You don't have to sacrifice practice of your present sport. Simply add half an hour a day to your schedule, put that half hour into serious walking, and you will have more stamina, strength, and quickness in your main sport. All it will cost you will be that half hour—a half hour, incidentally, that I believe you will soon come to find is most enjoyable in and of itself.

13

How Good Can You Get?

There is no way that any book can tell you how to reach your ultimate potential. Only years of experience plus advice from other walkers and coaches can do that for you. That's because the techniques of racewalking are infinitely perfectable. In a way the complexity of the sport is good news because it means that as you grow older you will not necessarily slow down a lot because your increasingly refined technique can make up for some of the inroads that aging must inevitably make.

All technique must start with the basic definition of racewalking according to international standards:

> Walking is progression by steps so taken that unbroken contact with the ground is maintained. At each step the advancing foot of the walker must make contact with the ground before the rear foot leaves the ground. During the period of each step when a foot is on the ground, the leg must be straightened at least for one moment, and in particular the supporting leg must be straight in the vertical upright position. (See TAC Rule 150, p. 158.)

You know that already. And you know that normal walking is the basis of racewalking, the major differences being in the ninety-degree bend at the elbow, in the locked knee and straightened leg, and in the hip girdle that gains you extra inches on each stride.

Up to this point, I have emphasized how simple walking is. However, the movements of walking are exceedingly complex. If you have ever tried to make a doll walk like a human being, you know a little of what I mean by complexity. The doll just doesn't look right.

You are in good company in not being able to reproduce the human style of walking in a nonhuman figure. The most skilled scientists have studied the subject and have been unable to come up with a robot that can walk in convincingly human fashion. I don't understand the complexities in any scientific way, and I am sure that you don't need to either.

You are working with an amazing piece of machinery when you take your body out for a walk. Take pride in that complexity and treat it right!

The Two-Stride Cycle

A walker's style is as unique as his fingerprints. There are correct principles to follow as you work toward perfecting your technique, but there is no one absolutely proper way. Everything you do, every trick you try, must be coordinated with the special strengths and weaknesses of your own system. As you study your technique, you must think of the whole pattern through a two-stride cycle. This takes you from the drive off one foot, the power shift to the other foot, and back to the position where the cycle started.

Obviously in the two-stride cycle (TSC) you will have two periods when both feet are touching the ground and two periods when only one foot is in contact. To improve most efficiently, you need to understand what happens in the TSC.

Go through the following movements slowly, concentrating on just what happens: Start with your arms at your sides and step forward with your left foot, toes pointing directly ahead. Reach out as far as you can with your hip and leg and plant your heel at about a 45-degree angle with the ground. The foot should be at a 90-degree angle with the leg, and the leg, of course, must be straight. As the back of your heel touches the ground, your ankle should be firmly in place so that the foot moves forward on the outside edge of your shoe. The foot is almost flat on the ground, but the outside edge is the side that transfers your weight from heel to toe.

You will be pulling your body forward with the left leg and at the same time pushing off with the right. Thus, during each TSC each leg alternately pulls and pushes your body forward, the changeover coming at that moment when your body is directly over the supporting leg.

When the leg is not pulling or pushing, it is swinging through the air, and in this phase it is important that the leg be relaxed. In fact, relaxation is a key to success in long-distance walking. If any muscles, even your facial ones, tighten up, that puts an unnecessary strain on your system and can throw your whole attempt at smoothness out of kilter.

Arm Action

Your hands should be loosely clenched, not squeezing hard. Your arm action will swing forward with the opposite leg. The arm must be bent at a right angle. This enables you to have a short, piston-like drive with each arm. The arms work as pendulums, and the longer the pendulum, the longer and slower the swing. By bending your arm to ninety degrees, you shorten the pendulum and permit yourself to speed up your arm strokes as you speed up the steps. (see Figure 3, p. 88).

The elbows should be close in to the body, just skimming your ribs as you drive through. The backward limit of this drive should bring your arm so high that the upper arm and shoulder form a nearly straight line. At the front end of the arm motion, your hand should cross no further than the middle of your body and no higher than the middle of your chest (see Figure 4).

Your body as a whole should be erect and as tall as you can make yourself. Racewalking will give you better posture because you will soon find that you walk better when your body is straight and reaching upward. Conversely, at the same time you will feel that you are getting down closer to the ground with your hips because the longer your stride, the lower to the ground you will be. But from the waist up, you must walk tall.

Your head always should face straight ahead. Never look down at yourself to see if your form is correct. If you can't find a partner to work with you, you'll have to settle for sensing how correct your style is, because the minute you look down to see, you will have ruined your style.

Proper Leg Action

Let's take a foot-to-head survey of some points that you can work on. First of all, the way you line up your feet as you walk is very important. The ideal way is to have each foot come down in a direct

Figure 3

Here is the short, piston-like drive with each arm. You can see from this why the upper body gets so much work in racewalking. What Kate needs to work on is more shoulder action along with the arms. Her right shoulder should come forward a couple of inches more to give her maximum drive from her arms.

Figure 4

Note that the feet land in a direct line and that the head is facing straight ahead. Try to avoid all motion that swings your body from one side to the other.

line, with this line passing through the middle of the foot. You may not have enough flexibility to do this (I don't), but it is a goal to work toward. You can practice this on a lonely road that has a center line or on a track. Simply hit the same line on each stride, and you're doing it properly. An acceptable second best is to have the inside of each foot hit the same imaginary line (see Figure 5).

Your feet should also land facing exactly in the direction you are heading. If you toe in or toe out, you can lose an inch or two on each stride. That doesn't sound like much until you realize that you take 1,300 or 1,400 strides each mile—suddenly thousands of inches sounds like a lot. And it is. So make sure your foot lands properly. It's also good protection against unnecessary injury.

Now for the supporting leg action. At the start of the support phase, your leg is just about fully straightened; the foot is at a 90-degree angle, and the outside corner of the heel makes first contact with the ground—at about a 45-degree angle. The ankle and knee are both locked to make a straight lever of the leg. As a lever, the leg is used to pull the body forward. Once the body is pulled over the leg, that leg starts its pushing propulsion from the drive off the toe (see Figure 6).

All this power can be utilized most effectively if you maintain contact with the ground with the trailing leg for as long as possible,

Figure 5

One of the easiest things for a partner to check is how well you manage to keep your perfect posture at the moment the weight of your body passes over the supporting foot. Note how Kate's body is in an absolutely straight line from her foot to her head.

Figure 6

Note that both legs are fully straightened at the moment when the outside corner of the heel makes first contact with the ground. The foot is at a 90-degree angle with the leg and at a 45-degree angle with the ground. The rear leg and toe are pushing the body forward, and the leading leg is about to start pulling the body forward.

thus lengthening the stride and increasing the power at the same time.

The Hip Girdle

As soon as the toe leaves the ground, the leg is no longer supplying any power. It now is the swing leg, and the knee leads the drive forward. The swing forward is done with the leg kept as low as possible to the ground, and as the swing leg reaches midpoint in the swing it begins to straighten. The hip is pushed forward, downward, and slightly to the side. Reach out as far ahead as possible to touch the heel down to the ground.

Obviously as the leg swings forward, the hip on that side also comes forward, pushing slightly downward as well. If the swing hip is pushed forward, the stride can be lengthened by as much as the hip goes forward, and this means as much as six inches added to the stride. There is some side-to-side movement of the hip, of course, but your goal should be to push the hip forward and gain these extra inches in stride. If you get the feeling that your hips are leading your body with the rest of you following, you'll be on the right track for proper hip action (see Figure 7).

Figure 7

Have your partner observe you from the rear to check on the hip girdle's effectiveness. Note that Kate has some hip movement to the side but that it is mostly a down-and-reaching-out movement that adds inches to her stride. Note also that the torso is straight along the whole backbone.

Your torso should be straight along the whole backbone. The only time this vertical position is changed is just past mid-stride when there may be a slight forward lean of the torso, no more than five degrees. Too much lean can cause creeping (failure to walk with a locked knee), and any back lean at all means a loss of both power and stride length.

The head, like the torso, should be erect and facing straight ahead. Carrying the head anywhere but absolutely in line with the torso, whether too far forward or too far backward, means that you will be affecting your balance, and balance and smoothness are the two keys to successful walking.

The Arms

The arms should work half like pendulums, half like pistons—that is, they should hang and swing naturally from the shoulders, but there should also be some power behind the swing. The degree to which you approach an all-out effort will determine how far back the arm swing goes. At the front, the ideal form for your arm swing is to cross the body no more than having your hand reach about the center of your body and to bring your arms up no higher than mid-chest. One way to improve the power you generate with your arms is to get your shoulders more into the act. Have your partner watch how far forward you are bringing your shoulders on each stride, and then have him or her go along beside you and hold a hand about two inches more in front of your shoulder. Then exaggerate the shoulder action until you touch your partner's hand with your shoulder, thus adding roughly two more inches of shoulder action to your form. It will feel awkward at first, but eventually you will be able to coordinate this extra shoulder action smoothly, and like the rest of your arm action, it will add to the length and power of your stride.

Quite obviously if you go out one day and attempt to incorporate all the suggestions of this chapter into one workout, you will be lucky not to fall down. Follow the suggestions one at a time. Decide, either alone or with your partner, that today you will concentrate on the foot plant, and do so. Then tomorrow you can work on the shoulder action. Try to bring the things into your act one by one, and constantly monitor yesterday's results today (see Figure 8).

You must do a great deal of thinking when you are learning to walk properly, but once you learn a technique, it will almost always stick with you for the simple reason that racewalking is the most

Figure 8

If you work with a partner, you can observe each other from the side and from the rear as you walk along, but it is also important occasionally to have each partner observe the other from directly ahead. Check for straightness of the torso, for the arms coming through close to the body, for the eyes straight ahead, for the hip girdle, and for the overall impression of smoothness and fluidity.

efficient way of moving along. Once your body learns a technique that makes walking easier, it's not likely to abandon it.

The ideas of this chapter can be worked on over a period of months. Don't try to rush things, and don't get discouraged. It's all going to pay off in the long run—or rather in the long walk.

When Should You Race?

*T*he question of when to start racing has many different answers, all of which depend on the personality of the individual walker. At one extreme, there is the person who simply is not competitive, who has taken up walking for the myriad other benefits, and who can answer this question without any help from me with a simple "Never!"

At the other extreme is the person like myself who dislikes spending even five minutes warming up for tennis, who wants to get to the enjoyment of competition as soon and as often as possible. Actually, the competitive people are of two totally different types—the easy losers and the fanatics. I'm of the easy loser type, and I went into my first walking race at a ridiculously long distance (forty kilometers) with practically no training other than having someone show me the basic technique. In addition, I was already in good shape from having run in the Boston Marathon a couple of months earlier.

I enjoyed that walk—most of it anyway—and finished eighth in a field of about fifteen. Clarence DeMar, a must-win type if there ever was one, also entered that race. He finished remarkably well for so old a man (well into his sixties) walking his first race. His secret was remarkably simple. He modified his running shuffle slightly and

94

jogged through the course. In the early going, some of the rest of us were moving along with him, and one veteran runner had the temerity to tell Mr. DeMar that his technique was of doubtful legality. (Actually, that was a lie; there was nothing doubtful about his style; Clarence was jogging.) All DeMar said was, "I'll wait till the judges tell me." And, of course, the rookie judge was not about to tell the great man anything. After all, DeMar had won the Boston Marathon eight times, and that was enough qualification for accepting his new walking style.

If you are like DeMar and unable to accept defeat gracefully under any terms, you should be careful about when you make your racing debut. Have a trial workout at least ten days before the proposed race. Ask a knowledgeable person where you can expect to finish with a time like that of your workout, and if you can't accept that result as a satisfactory debut in racing, go on with your training a while more.

If you are really intense about your competitive career, delay it for at least six months after the start of your training and make sure that your first race is at least four miles long and no longer than twenty kilometers. The reason is that at shorter distances your body exerts itself too hard for a short period, somewhat like sprinting for a runner. At the longer distances, there are simply too many possibilities of injury through over-exertion. So stick to the middle ranges for your first races. Fortunately, these are the most common distances in racewalking, so if you can find any races close to home, chances are that you will find one of a distance between four and twelve miles.

On the other hand, if you are easy-going, easily amused, and fond of competing whether you win or lose (of course, you always want to win, but you're not a crier, furniture-buster, or sulker when you lose), then you can hardly get into a race too soon. If you enter a distance for which you have never before timed yourself, have someone follow you and don't feel that it is a test of your manliness (or your feminity, for that matter) for you to finish.

I admit that I admire the individuals who never quit, who drive themselves to near disaster every time they race. But I also kind of admire my own attitude, which is to have fun through my sport. For me, finishing a race with bleeding blisters, vomiting guts, or a splitting headache is just not fun, and I quit when things get too bad.

There's a battle going on between your body and your brain each time you go all out in a race or in training. Your body tells you to take it easy, that it's going to get hurt, that there's always tomorrow when the body will feel more like it. Your body is a natural conservative that wants to be ready for some unexpected emergency waiting around the corner. Your body is basically lazy.

Well, you have to accept your body as a partner in this matter of walking fast, but you have to keep in control with your mind and spirit. If you think of yourself as a jockey on a horse in a big race, you have a good idea of the relationship between your desire for victory and your body's reluctance to go along with that desire.

No jockey wants to ruin a horse for the next race, but when the race is on the line, when it's a matter of victory or defeat, the jockey takes out the whip and lambasts the horse. That's what you have to do to your body. Push it. Don't let it tell you that it can't do something until you have tried. At the same time, don't force your body to the point at which some terrible injury takes place and you are laid up for a week or month or whatever.

Like everything else in racewalking, no one can put down exact rules as to how hard you can force your body before the forcing becomes counterproductive. Only you can figure this out for yourself by experimenting.

Thus, training at fast speeds becomes vital. Unless you have lots of races in your neighborhood, you must duplicate in training what you would face in a race. That's why interval training is so important to your improvement. If you are doing intervals, you are going even faster than you will go in a race. Of course, you are going only a fraction of the race distance, but through the many repetitions you are getting experience not only in speed but also in forcing your body to do what it starts complaining about. And from the interval workouts you will find just when you must listen to your body's complaints and when you can safely ignore them.

Early morning workouts will also give you experience in learning how far you can trust your body. Almost every body will tell its brain that it needs another half hour's sleep. But when you force your body out of bed, into walking clothes, and out into nature, you will usually find that your entire being enjoys the experience of being up before the rest of the world. Everything is extra beautiful early in the morning, and you can usually say to your body, "See! I told you so. Walking really is great at this time of day."

Achieving a Balance

I'm only being half-facetious about the mind-body conflict. It is extremely important that you achieve a balance between your goals and your abilities. If you drive yourself unrealistically, you will end by hurting yourself. Walking is the safest sport there is, but even in walking you can hurt yourself if you drive yourself unmercifully and go far beyond what your body is ready for. On the contrary, if you never push yourself beyond what is easy for you, you will quickly find a level of achievement that never improves, and you will be a life-long back-of-the-pack walker.

There is a fine line between too much and too little training. You're going to be your own coach, and if you plan to come anywhere near your potential, you must constantly search for that fine line, and then walk it.

The Basis of Walking

Racing is not the basis for your walking career, however, even though races may become what you aim for and what you talk about in social circles. Training is the basis, the daily bread and butter. Still, because the incentive factor is so vital to long-term success in walking, at least for the truly competitive types among us, it is important that you plan your races carefully.

Some people can race so often that in many big city areas a walker who also runs can almost make races his training, entering both walking and running races each week. My own approach is to do my running here on Cape Cod, where there are lots of races, and to do my traveling once a month or less for the walks. If there were walking races, I would never have to run a race. But there aren't, and I do like competition so I enter the running events.

I learned that, for me personally, running and walking mix fairly well. In 1964, I was more serious about walking than I have ever been at any other point in my career. For months through the winter I did no running but concentrated on walking, aiming at the fifty-kilometer event in the Tokyo Olympics. I did distance, intervals, everything as best I knew how at the time.

But when spring rolled around bringing with it the big pre-Boston Marathon races around the city, I suddenly had an urge to compete. The first race was what we called the Greek race. It started at historic Lexington Green and ended at a Greek Orthodox church in Central Square in Cambridge, nine miles away. I went mainly for the social aspects and had a fine time before the race started, greeting old friends.

As I said, it was a big race in those days, meaning that maybe seventy-five runners showed up for it. I stayed in the middle of the pack at the start, moving easily and expecting nothing from the race. Then at about two miles I realized that I felt good and that I was still in sight of the leaders. I counted places and found that I was in fifteenth place, a good spot for a runner like me. I got a bit excited at that point and moved up a couple of notches, moving too fast too early as was usual for me, but even at the end of the race I was still doing far better than I had expected and I finished thirteenth and felt great.

In other words, I had trained strictly on walking and yet my running came out as good as it ever had in years when I had concentrated on running.

Although I was slightly ill the day of the Boston Marathon and didn't do much, about six weeks later I had a great day at the Yonkers (N.Y.) Marathon, still running on the training I had done by walking.

Yonkers was an Olympic trial that year, with the winner guaranteed the final spot on that year's team, two other places having already been settled. The day was brutally hot, and as it was an out-and-back course I got to see some famous runners, many of them obviously in difficulty. I trotted along at my own pace, moving up all the way, and at the end I was in eleventh place, the sixth American in an Olympic trial. Of course, my time was around 3:15, and the winner and qualifier for Tokyo was about forty minutes ahead of me, but I was still the happiest eleventh-place finisher in Yonkers history. (Eleventh was traditionally the moaner's spot at Yonkers because there were always ten good watches as prizes and then twenty identical medals for finishing eleventh through thirtieth.) Thus, I had run one of the most successful races of my career, and I had done my training almost exclusively in walking.

Races Are Fun

But I am wandering from the point of this chapter, which is to tell you that races are fun, win or lose, if you have the right attitude. It's worth traveling a hundred miles for a race (although my wife would offer a strong rebuttal to that statement if I let her). It's good fun if you can get a friend to travel with you. The friend either can be a fellow walker or someone who will act as your trainer during the race, giving you water and encouragement in equal doses. One of each, a fellow walker and a waterboy, would be the ideal traveling team, of course.

Incidentally, if you are fortunate enough to have a friend passing out water to you during a race, be sure to tell that friend to give the same aid to your competitors. Nothing sours a new walker's reputation faster than to see someone give water to one thirsty soul and then turn away from the next equally desperate walker. We're all friends in walking; it's really a great society, and to be part of it, you must learn to share.

Here then are the things you need to keep in mind when you plan on starting a career in actual races:

1. Find out where and when the races are being held. Contact your local chapter of the Walkers Club of America, the TAC, or the Road Runners Club. Local athletic clubs, largely made up of runners, also usually will be able to put you in contact with any individuals who racewalk in your area.

2. Make sure you can go the distance of the race. Take a trial walk of at least that much distance a couple of weeks before the race.

3. Try to talk your walking friends into entering the race with you. Two neophytes can support each other. In the race, walk together at first at a seemingly easy pace. You'll still probably be going too fast because you'll be so excited.

4. Prepare for the race with common sense, nothing more. Just pretend that the race is merely a time trial in your overall training schedule. Actually that's all it is. Eat and rest sensibly, just as you always do. Don't attempt any pre-race carbo loading, coffee drinking, or anything of that sort. You'll only upset your system if you try to get fancy.

5. Arrive at the race in time to go through a good warmup. You probably will be excited, and the adrenalin will take care of much of your warmup requirements, but it's still a good idea to do a few minutes of exercises (if you're an exerciser) and at least a half mile of walking, gradually working up to race pace. This warmup will help you make sure that your shoes won't come untied, your socks won't bunch up, and nothing else will go wrong right at the start.

6. In the race, walk at your own pace. You will be tempted to go very fast for a short while, but if you do, you'll pay for it later. Start with the conservative pace you would use for a training session at the same distance. When the butterflies have winged their way out of your system, you can then pick up the pace if it is too slow. One reason it's better to start too slowly than too fast is that it's psychologically much better to pass other walkers during a race than to have them pass you.

7. If any veteran walker has been pointed out to you as just about your speed, walk with that person. The veterans seldom do foolish things. Similarly, if you find yourself walking near an older walker during the first third of a race, stay with him or her for a while. You will have time to move ahead during the later stages if you

really are stronger, and if you aren't, hanging on will bring you along just a bit faster than you would have done on your own.

8. The main rule to follow during a race is a flexible one: Keep on the lookout for ways to enjoy the race. Walking is a pleasure, and the races should be a key part of that pleasure. Of course, in the final stages of any race you are going to be pushing hard enough to hurt a bit, but it doesn't last for long, and the feeling at the end when you know you've given your best makes up for any pain you forced on yourself.

Believe me, races really are fun!

15

What Is a Walking Race Like?

Walking races are as different from one another as the people who organize them, but along with the differences there are certain things you can count on in a good race. For one thing, because racewalking has not yet reached the state of big money-making the way running has, I almost can guarantee that the race will be organized by a racewalker, not a fast-buck promoter. This means that the athlete, not some sponsoring organization, is going to be considered first, and that in turn means that the water stations will be at the most helpful places, the course will be a pleasant one, and the pre- and post-race treatment will be well-intentioned if not always efficient.

An added benefit to the best races is that they tend to be held at the same time of the year, year after year, and this means that you know what to expect and get to compete against your own times of previous years. There's no better feeling than knowing that you have walked a personal record.

In New England, the best and oldest race is the Taunton twenty-kilometer walk, traditionally·held on the hottest day of the summer. It's usually a July race, and of the twenty-six years that it's been held, the temperature in the shade has been closer to ninety than to seventy in about twenty of those years.

One characteristic that Taunton shares with just about every walking race is that the size of the field will be downright chummy compared to what you find in a running race. If fifty walkers show up at Taunton, that's a banner year. In some years—1983, for example—there are more trophies (thirty-five) than finishers (twenty-eight). One year, I brought along a new friend who was a pretty good walker and a better runner. He had just moved to New England from California, and I didn't know him well, but on the drive from Cape Cod to Taunton we became better acquainted. Among other things, he told me that he had run a marathon four times and had broken three hours three times. As he also had a fairly good racewalking style, I knew he would do well at Taunton, and I was correct. He came in seventh, five minutes ahead of me. (My daughter also beat me by one minute that day. She was eleventh; I was twelfth.)

On the way home, Jeff was very excited by his trophy. He told us that this was the first trophy he had ever won. He had nothing to show for all his races as a runner in spite of all the talent that he so obviously had. He was converted to racewalking from running on the basis of how much easier it was to win a prize in a walk.

It reminded me of the way running races used to be in New England. Starting in 1947, I successfully competed as a runner for years and won several hundred trophies and medals even though I was never more than fairly good. The fields in races other than the Boston Marathon in the old days (up to the late 1960s) were usually less than fifty, just as in walking races today.

Walking is thus still a fairly exclusive thing. I like that. I miss being "different" the way I was in my first twenty years of running. The small fields mean one additional benefit for the racewalker compared to the runner: You get to talk to and be friends with the famous walkers, not just with those of your own ability. In my days as a so-so runner, I was good friends with both Johnny Kelleys, Jock Semple, and just about every American who finished in the top ten at Boston over a twenty-year period. What middle-of-the-pack runner can say that today?

Racewalkers are still that way. At one time or another, the Taunton race has attracted just about every top American walker. We all know each other. All the Rons have been there—Laird,

Daniels, Kulik, and the great Ron Zinn, who still holds the record. Zinn was the first American to attain international stature in modern times, finishing sixth in the Tokyo Olympics among other things. A West Point graduate, he was killed in Vietnam before he had a chance to show what his true potential might have been.

Taunton also attracts some real characters. For example, there was Charley who got up early on the morning of the race one year and walked twenty miles to the race from his home near Providence. It didn't hurt him in the race either. In 1983, Dennis Childs, one of the better young walkers in New England, decided to make the race day one of exercise, so he hopped on his bicycle in Springfield that morning and pedalled 104 miles, arriving at Taunton just a few minutes before the race started. Unlike Charley, Dennis showed the effects of his lengthy warmup, but he still finished well up in the top half of the field that day even if he was not among the top contenders as he usually is.

The success of the Taunton race has occurred because of what race director Win Benton calls "an ideal combination of worker and organizer." Benton is the worker. Al White of the Taunton American Legion was the original organizer, cajoling and bullying his fellow Legionnaires into backing the race. Benton does the rest. He contacts the walkers, sets out the course, goes around town and gets people to volunteer to finance a trophy, buys the trophies, and then acts as starter, chief timer, and head walking judge of the race. His wife, Gladys, helps in everything and sees to it that the race concludes with the beef stew that used to be traditional at the Boston Marathon before the field became too unwieldly and they had to go to containers of yogurt.

Al White has since died, but Chuck White, no relation, is now the Legion commander, and he sees to it that the Bentons get the organizational support they need to carry on the race. In 1983, for example, Benton was seriously ill, having recently had a leg amputated below the knee. He felt that there would be no Taunton race that year, a pity because it was the twenty-fifth anniversary of the race. Then, somehow, people from Taunton and from among the walkers themselves came up with half a dozen workers, just about enough to do the things that Benton did by himself in other years, and the race went on.

Taunton has always been my favorite race, and as a result I have missed only three of the twenty-six. That means that I can compare my efforts each year to those of the past, and that in turn means that 1983 was a really exciting year for me because it happened to hit one of those days on which everything went well, and I finished fourth in 1:54:13. The three ahead of me were Bob Keating, Tom Knatt, and Bob Falciola, all present or former New England champions and Taunton winners, and although I was well out of sight of third place, the result was enough to keep me on a cloud of happiness for days after.

More than finishing fourth, however, was the pleasure of comparing 1983, when I was fifty-nine, to some of my previous results. For one thing, it was the first time since 1975 that I had broken two hours, and while the 1:54 was almost ten minutes off my all-time best set in 1963, it was only two minutes off my 1967 time. To have slipped only two minutes in sixteen years is the kind of silver lining that fading racewalkers keep searching for in the cloudy days of old age.

I have already stressed the fact that racewalking is a sport that one can carry on for a lifetime, but the Taunton twenty-kilometer race offers spectacular proof that the older walker cannot merely keep on at a feeble pace but can actually compete on a high level. The proof is the fact that all but three of the former winners over the twenty-six years of the race are still competing successfully enough to be mentioned from time to time in the *Ohio Racewalker* for finishing in the top five of some race somewhere.

These veteran walkers include England's gift to American racewalking, John Knifton, a Taunton winner in the 1960s and still one of the USA's top master racewalkers; Long John Kelly, originally from Ireland, another 1960s winner, another master champion today; and Shaul Ladany from Israel, still a super long-distance walker for whom the twelve-mile distance at Taunton is just a sprint. Incidentally, Kelly is called "Long John" to distinguish him from the two John Kelleys, "The Younger" and "The Elder," who are former Boston marathon winners. I finished eleventh in the American national marathon championship in 1964 at Yonkers, and the two Kelleys and Long John were ahead of me, first, sixth, and ninth. Like me and many others, Long John has since turned more and more to walking and less to running.

One of the early women's racewalkers I have told you about was held annually in conjunction with the twenty-kilometer men's race. The distaff race had fields of as many as a dozen girls, but the sport never caught on, and after five years it was dropped. Today New England women walkers like Chris Anderson or my own daughter Kate are well able to compete with the men; twenty years ago we all felt that the limit for girls was probably around five miles and thus they needed to have their own race.

In any case, it has turned out that women, like men, can go on to long careers in walking. One of the Taunton five milers was won by Jeannie Bocci of Michigan. She and her racewalking husband heard about Taunton, and they packed their Volkswagen bus with the racewalking girls that they were introducing to the sport in Michigan, and the busload showed up at Taunton for the race. Jeannie won the women's race easily; the younger girls did well; and Jeannie's husband, Gerry, finished well up among the men in the longer race.

I still read about Jeannie Bocci winning races almost twenty years later. I know that my own two daughters, who competed at Taunton, still enter a walking race occasionally and do well. Kate has been the first woman in the New England thirty-kilometer race on two occasions, and Linda finished second in the national two-mile indoor racewalking championship for submasters in 1981. Women, like men, can keep on as racewalkers almost indefinitely, and that is one of the pleasures of going to a walking race: You know that you're going to be coming back year after year.

Getting to the Race

One of the most difficult things is learning when a race will take place. It is thus vital that you make contact with the TAC office for your association. TAC associations correspond roughly to states, but there are sixty TACs in all. Some of them, like New England, cover more than one state (Massachusetts, Rhode Island, New Hampshire and Vermont), others cover individual states (Connecticut and Maine), and many of them cover a part of a state (West Texas, Southwestern, South Texas, Border, and Gulf Associations for Texas, for example).

Each TAC has an association representative for racewalking, and that person will be the one for you to contact to keep posted about races. When the TAC representative tells you of a race, apply for an entry blank and send it back to the race director. Then show up on the day of the race, preferably at least a half hour ahead of race time.

Tom Knatt of Concord, Massachusetts, the man who has won more New England titles than any individual in recent history, is famous for cutting things close when it comes to making a race on time. I especially remember the 1971 Taunton race. I was one of a group of four walkers moving out together through the early miles. I was trying not to get too excited at the prospect of winning the race, but I knew I had a real chance because the other three were all roughly equal in ability to me. Then at two miles, Win Benton drove up and informed us that Tom Knatt had arrived at the start four minutes after the field had taken off. Knatt was coming, and our hopes were going. Tom was so clearly the class of the field that he caught us well before the halfway mark and coasted to one of his three wins in the race while I settled for third. Knatt, incidentally, is another bit of living proof of the longevity of racewalkers because he has continued at a high level since that 1971 victory, and in 1983, for example, he finished second in the race in time as fast as he had done twelve years earlier.

The Day of the Race

But you're going to get to the race ahead of time. You pick up your number at the desk and pay the entry fee if you haven't already done so. (At Taunton there is no fee. The sponsoring American Legion picks up the tab and no one is looking to make a profit. Again that's the way road races in running were held in New England prior to the boom. No one ever thought of making money on running.)

Next, you dress for the race, or perhaps you already dressed at home. Whereas runners almost always have to dress at home because of the confusion at the race, walkers will find plenty of room to dress at the race site and to shower afterwards.

Once dressed, go out on the street and do your warming up. If you have any questions about style, this is the time to ask them. A great champion like Ron Laird will be glad to give you advice. I never asked a top racewalker for help without being given at least a friendly helpful answer. Furthermore, if you're too shy to approach the star walkers and ask for help, simply by being out there and warming up you'll more than likely find someone coming up to you and making suggestions as to subtle changes that you should try. Knatt, Jack Boitano, Bob Falciola, and Paul Schell, all one-time Taunton winners, have volunteered helpful advice to me at one or more times over the years, without my ever asking for it.

As you move up and down the street, working on your style during the warmup, making sure that your clothing and shoes are comfortable, you'll see others doing the same thing. You won't have to be an expert to tell which walkers have the best style; a good racewalker glides along in silky smooth fashion that no longer looks the least bit ridiculous once the barest rudiments of the style have been mastered.

Some minor local dignitary will probably be there to start you off, and the race will quickly develop into several races within a race. The top walkers will form their own little group before you have gone around the first two corners at Taunton—and those corners come in the first 300 yards. There will be a second group of good-but-conservative walkers, and a third group whose average pace even at the start will be little faster than twelve minutes a mile. Whatever your own ability, you'll find other walkers in the field with whom to compete.

The Race Begins

The danger at the start of a race is too much excitement. You'll have so much adrenalin flowing through your system that a pace a good minute a mile faster than what you're used to will seem easy. That is, it will seem easy for a mile or two. Then you'll find yourself exhausted with ten miles to go.

The way to combat this tendency to ruin your race through too fast an early pace is to talk to other walkers before the race. Tell them what you are hoping to average per mile for the race and ask which of the other walkers are likely to go at about that pace. Then select the oldest of the walkers who are pointed out as being roughly in your class and promise yourself that you won't go ahead of that person for at least a mile.

You'll start off at what may seem to you to be a ridiculously slow pace. Everything will be so easy that you'll have to fight the tendency not to wait for a full mile before moving up. At the end of the mile, you may still feel that way, but it's much more likely that once the euphoria and the adrenalin wear off, you'll find that the "slow" pace setter you've been following suddenly seems to be going much faster. By the end of twelve miles, you may not even be able to keep up with him.

What if you follow a walker at a too-slow pace for that first mile? It's hardly a fatal error. You still have eleven miles to make up for whatever ground you have lost. (I'm using the Taunton distance for my example, but it's the ratio that counts. If you are in a five-mile race, keep conservative for a half a mile; if it's a twenty-mile race, don't get too frisky for a couple of miles.) The other thing about a comparatively slow start is the psychological factor. If you are moving up in a race, going past other walkers, that's a nice psychological boost; but if you go out too fast and after a while others start passing you, that's depressing even though you may actually be at the same point in the field as you would have been if you had started slowly and moved up.

One other way that you will benefit from entering a race is the fact that there will be a judge observing your technique. Every walker has to wonder whether or not his racing style is legal. It's a good feeling to have a judge nod approval or, as Win Benton does, actually say, "You look good, John." If you are close to illegality, many judges will tell you what you're doing wrong. "This isn't a warning," they may say, "but you need to. . . ."

In the latter stages of a race, you will have to make your own way. There is no way that a book can tell you how to have a more determined attitude, how to raise your pain threshold, or how to keep your form. There's no strategy. You simply decide how much pain you want to endure (I'm not big on that myself) and how much difference a minute or two in your total time matters (I tend to try to get away from other walkers before the last mile, either by trying to fake them out and moving away or by letting them get ahead of me so I won't be tempted into a last-minute race to the finish line). If you end up in a close race to the finish, be sure to remember that there is no second warning in the final quarter mile of a race. If you are given a warning in that stretch drive, you are disqualified. You may have had perfect form for eleven-plus miles, but if you break stride (and get caught) in the final sprint, you lose everything except a DQ beside your name in the final results. I've seen some very angry, disappointed top walkers in that situation. Don't let it happen to you.

After the Race Is Over

One of the best parts of a race, especially at Taunton, is the post-race socializing. And one of the nice things for me about walking is that even after a hard race I'm able to eat well. After a running race, my stomach can hardly take more than a couple of mouthfuls. I theorize that the difference is that the runner's stomach has been jounced up and down for miles, while the walker's stomach has stayed on the level as the body glides along.

Anyway, I enjoy the socializing after the Taunton race or after any walk. The group is small enough to fit comfortably in one large room. It's nice to be able to hobnob with the winner. And most of all, walkers are still different enough so that you find some really delightful characters among them.

Runners today seem so humorlessly intent on doing the "right" thing—discussing shoes; diet; strategy; interval training versus long, slow distance; best stop watches and other devices; and all the other things that fill all those issues of magazines year after year—that they seem to have lost much of the joy of their sport. I've seen runners quite depressed because they can't seem to achieve a runner's high—whatever that is. (I've never known it either, but it doesn't depress me.) I don't think that racewalkers have yet fooled themselves into that near-religious belief in a "high," but I do know that I've had a great deal of good, low-class pleasure from my thousands of miles of walking.

Anyway, a good part of that pleasure is in getting to know the walkers over a glass of beer after a race. Don't tell your wife or husband that you'll be home soon after the race. Give yourself an hour or two to unwind and to enjoy belonging to a special society after the race is over.

If you've done well, it's fun to talk about it. If you've had a disappointing race, it's therapeutic to talk about it with others who have gone through the same thing and who can tell you how to go about doing better the next time.

Your Competitors

Walkers are so disparate a group that it's hard to pick out one and say that he or she is typical. In New England's little circle, for example, we have factory workers, teachers, computer experts, a couple of doctors, a retired radio station engineer, a plumber, a truck driver, a railroad worker, an ice man, salesmen, office workers, and a couple of unemployable types.

If anyone represents the spirit of true amateurism, however, it's Fred Brown, and with athletes in general making so much money today, racewalkers are close to the last remaining bastion of true amateurism. (We don't really want it that way; we just don't have any financial offers to lead us astray.)

In many ways, Fred Brown's career is much like my own except that Fred has done everything longer, more often, and generally better than I ever did. Like me, Fred was a runner for years before he discovered racewalking. Actually he was involved in many other sports before he discovered running in 1934 at the age of thirty. (And if you want to hear about longevity in sports, Fred had his name in the *Boston Globe* for three straight weeks in 1984 for finishing fifth each time in the weekly five-mile walks held in Lowell, pretty good for a 79-year-old. The other side of the story is that there were only five competitors in the race each time, but that doesn't negate the fact that Fred walked and finished all three races.)

Fred was never a great runner or great walker. His best finish in Boston was twenty-third and his fastest time was 3:00:30. His most quoted achievement during his running days was a joke that Boston reporters took literally. The great Tarzan Brown, the Boston Marathon favorite that year, had had a bad race and was nowhere to be seen among the top finishers. The reporters asked Fred where Tarzan (no relative) was, and Fred said, "Oh, he got sick of running and took a swim in Lake Cochituate" (at the ten-mile mark). You can still read in histories of the Boston Marathon that Tarzan Brown quit the race that year when he was among the leaders and jumped into the lake. It supposedly shows what a carefree spirit Tarzan was. Well, Tarzan was carefree all right, a wonderful man Fred tells me, but he wasn't casual about his sport. Unlike most badly beaten favorites, Tarzan kept right on going even though he had all sorts of problems that day, and he finished far, far down among the also-rans. Fred beat him and to this day he admires Tarzan for having the determination to finish like an ordinary semi-competent, but Fred's casual remark about the mythical swim—Fred seldom tells anything in a straightforward way—has become a permanent part of sports apocrypha.

There's no need to exaggerate or be whimsical to show what a career Fred has had, however. Perhaps he is proudest of having won several team prizes with his brothers Frank and Graham. This was in the 1930s, when team competition in New England was taken seriously. The Brown success as a team was based on the fact that Frank was a top runner, Fred was good, and Graham managed to finish.

Fred always enjoyed his running, but he also had many physical problems. After he discovered racewalking in 1949, he turned more and more to that sport, and for the last twenty years he has concentrated on walking. Proof that old age has failed to keep him from success are the prizes he has won as close to 200 of his collection of over 800 medals have come from walks, dozens of them won since he turned sixty.

If you make it to a walking race in New England, you're almost certain to meet Fred. He seldom misses one, showing up to work as an official if the distance is too much for him. You won't find him very often at the races of other TAC associations, but there is something about the challenge of racewalking that attracts interesting characters, and whenever you race, I predict that you'll find yourself involved with some fascinating personalities. As I've said, the people you meet are one of the nice bonus features of racewalking.

TAC Associations

The best way to meet these interesting people is to go to races, and the best way to find out where the races are is to contact your TAC/USA office. Most TAC associations not only have races that are fixtures like the Taunton race in New England but also sponsor annual championships such as five-, ten-, fifteen-, and so on up to fifty-kilometer races. These are run at different sites each year to give everyone an equal opportunity to compete without traveling too far. The same is true of the national TAC championships. The only way to keep up with all this is to contact the TAC office for your geographic area. The office will send you a list of all the walking races for the year in that association. In states like California, New Jersey, New York, Ohio, Maine, Wisconsin, and the Washington, D.C., area, the lists will be long. Even in those associations in which racewalking is just getting a foothold, so to speak, there will probably be racewalking clinics, and these are at least as important as the races are for neophytes.

The main thing is that you want to keep in touch, and the TAC office is the place to start.

16

What Do You Do When You Can't Find a Race?

*R*ight now I'm looking at a list of walking races for a one-month period in the United States. There are races in Arkansas; California; Colorado; Connecticut; Washington, D.C.; Georgia; Hawaii; Iowa; Indiana; Massachusetts; Michigan; Missouri; Nebraska; New Jersey; New York; Ohio; Oregon; Rhode Island; Tennessee; Virginia; and Washington.

That's impressive, but the list includes only twenty-two states, leaving twenty-eight without any racewalking activities during this particular month. Maybe a few states had races that escaped notice, but even so, there are wide areas in this country with no races in any given month. The chances are good that you're going to be ready for competition before there is any ready nearby for you.

One suggestion that I've already mentioned is to get into a running race and see how many triumphs you can score by walking faster than someone else can run. That's fun, but it also means starting dead last in a field of hundreds and then finishing far behind the leaders, being content with beating a few stragglers.

If you want a walking race, and there aren't any for hundreds of miles from your home, what do you do? The answer is to start your own race. To have a race, the basic requirements are an organizer, a field of walkers, and a judge.

Well, you are going to be the organizer, and if you have a couple of friends in training, then you also have the basis of a field. Talk a couple of trophy-starved runners into trying your sport (a trophy makes an unbelievably cheap bribe), and you're ready to go.

Informal Races

I hope that you will have informal races with your friends now and then. These can be set up during a practice outing when one of you says, "I really feel good today," and the other says, "Me, too." Then one of you says, "Let's move for the last mile," and you start picking up the pace, and the next thing you know it's a race back to the start.

If the walkers are of unequal abilities, the race has to be a handicap affair with one of you getting a head start and the other trying to catch up before a certain point.

But the races I'm talking about in this chapter are real ones, races set up weeks in advance. These should have maximum publicity, trophies, careful timing, judges, and refreshments afterwards.

Involving Other Walkers

The first thing to do is to make sure that at least a couple of others will take part with you. If you are in an area where racewalking is new, they will become not only the committee but also the field.

Next, decide on a distance. Somewhere around five miles makes a good start, because it's long enough so the stylistic offenders who may show up will burn themselves out before a judge has to throw them out. If you only get a half dozen people to come, you really don't want to disqualify any of them. On the other hand, you don't want an illegal walker to win. Five miles will usually take care of any well-intentioned but ignorant walkers. Anything much longer than five miles, however, will mean that your chances of attracting a good field will be drastically reduced.

For example, I have organized a thirty-kilometer walk down here on the Cape for the past ten years. The old standbys of New England walking show up, and we have a pleasant reunion back at my house after the race, but because of the distance the race has been practically worthless in getting new walkers involved in the sport. Perhaps four or five individuals have tried the thirty-kilometer during one or more of those ten years. And I don't mean four or five people in one year; I mean four or five for a total of ten years. If my race were meant to help start walking on Cape Cod, it would have been a terrible failure as almost all the successful walkers have been from off-Cape, the exceptions being myself, my daughter, and two fellow teachers at the school where I taught.

So, you plan a five-mile course. This course should be as simple as possible because nothing ruins a race faster than having part of the field lose its way. An out-and-back course down one road for two and a half miles has obvious advantages; so does a repeating course over a two-mile lap three times. Whatever your course may be, mark the road with chalk before the race starts, and take the walkers for a ride over the course just before race time.

Publicity

As soon as you know what your date and course will be—and for the date, study the local running race schedule and avoid conflict, thus making it possible for your race to pick up a few runners—let the newspapers know about it. Big-city dailies won't give you space, but local papers will be delighted with a new sport to cover. (I know, because my daughter and I are the sports writers for *The Cape Codder*, a local twice-a-week paper. Whenever anyone gives us information about a new event, we're always happy to pass that information on to our readers. Then we get out and cover it with camera and pencil.)

If you inform all the papers within a ten-mile radius, you may well pick up a few entries from comparatively nearby walkers whose existence you never even suspected. You can run off entry blanks at practically no cost if you know someone who works in a school, a church, an office with a copier, or a library. You probably won't need many blanks anyway. After all, we're talking about setting up a race in an area where walking is a little-known activity.

On the other hand, if you are interested in setting up a big race in an active walking area, there is only one way to go about it. Seek out an established race and volunteer to work on that. You will be welcome because workers always are, and the things you learn from the experience of others will hold you in good stead when it comes to having a race of your own. It will also give you contacts for helpers on your own race. Because of the comparative dearth of walking races, you will find walkers most cooperative when it comes to managing races.

Judging

Judging is like walking itself: It's an infinitely perfectable art, and an Olympic judge has all sorts of momentous decisions to make, but it's also a fairly simple thing to do at the starting level. This is because a good walker will look as though he's walking, and the nonwalkers simply won't look right.

Because all you want to do in your first race is make sure that the winner and one or two others at least are walking fairly, all your neophyte judge will have to do is to keep after the ones who look as though they aren't walking. Tell the judge to use phrases like, "Straighten your leg every stride or I'll have to give you a warning." "This isn't a warning, but you're going so fast that you're leaving the ground every stride. Slow down so I don't have to give you a warning." "You're bouncing up and down. Slow down and get smooth. You'll finish stronger and I won't have to give you a warning."

This is tantamount to coaching, and it's exactly what a judge should be doing in a race like yours.

Your judge could be a wife (mine has spotted some quite subtle illegalities over the years, although she's never been an actual judge); an old-timer (your newspaper publicity may well bring out a person who walked in races years ago); an injured walker (I keep saying that you never get injured in walking, but walkers do have automobile accidents, poison ivy, burns, blisters, and colds, so you have a chance of finding one laid up on the day of your race); or a person who has acted as an official in almost any other sport (because just as important as recognizing the faults of illegal walking is the authoritativeness to put the message across to the sinner in such a way that he or she either changes style or at least slows down and doesn't embarrass everyone by finishing among the leaders).

You now have a race course, a date and time, a judge, and a field of a few walkers. (I've had as few as eight enter my thirty-kilometer walk, and the year of only eight was one of the best walks ever because three different walkers had the lead at one time or another during the second half of the race.) You are ready.

The newspaper publicity should emphasize that post entries will be accepted, and you thus may add a couple of more entries on the day of the race.

Checklist

To make the race go smoothly, here is what you need to have:

Two or more stop watches should be on hand plus two or more people to run them. One watch should be used at the one- and three-mile stations, and the other at the two- and four-mile stations. (Of course, check beforehand that the two watches time equally.) Both watches should be there for the finish.

You will need numbers and four pins per number. You may know every walker by sight, but the numbers tell the people who see you all go past that this is indeed an official race. Getting the public accustomed to recognizing walking as a real sport is part of the growth process in building up the sport as an accepted one.

You will need trophies, including six for the first three male and female finishers plus age-group trophies for walkers who are over forty and under sixteen. If you know you're going to get a couple of walkers who are over fifty or sixty or under twelve, be sure to have trophies for these categories too.

Sure, the race is going to cost you some money. If you have ten trophies at an average of $5 each, that's $50 right there. I would suggest that you go a step further and offer a trophy to everyone who you know will be in the race. If you charge a $4 entry fee and then buy small trophies after the top few, you won't be much in the hole, and if you think in terms of what you would have to pay if you went to a golf course for eighteen holes, the few bucks it costs you to put on a race won't seem bad at all.

Provide food for the walkers after the race. Because you're not likely to get even as many as twenty walkers for this first race, you can afford to invite them all back to your house for a snack. Walkers can eat a lot, so be prepared. Beer and soft drinks are a starter, plus sandwich makings of cold cuts, salad fixings, potato chips, and the like. Ice-cream bars make a simple tasty dessert. Have a big pot of coffee, too.

You also should have some liquid refreshments at some point during the race. If you use the suggested out-and-back course, a card table with drinks on it in the middle of the course will serve double duty. The walkers will pass it on the way out and on the way back.

Here are a few other hints:

Measuring your course by automobile is all right, but if you can't check the odometer against a carefully measured mile, you should measure with two different cars and take the average of the two or even bring in a third vehicle if the disparity between the first two is too great.

Make it clear that your race will be held regardless of the weather. Walking can be done quite well under just about any conditions short of a major blizzard or flood, and braving the elements will make your walkers a little bit extra proud of themselves. It will also add to the impressiveness of the whole show in terms of letting the public know that walking is a sport with a difference.

Have all walkers sign a release, with parents signing for minors. It should read like this:

> In consideration of this entry being accepted, I hearby for myself and my heirs, executors and administrators waive and release any and all rights and claims for damages I may have against the (name of race), the T.A.C., the race sponsors, race officials, and the town of _____, for any and all injuries or damages suffered by me in connection with this event. I also verify that I am properly trained to compete at this distance.

SIGNATURE IN FULL _____ DATE _____
PARENT'S SIGNATURE (if under 18) _____

If any organization helps you with prizes, refreshments, volunteer workers, or in any other way, be sure that credit for all such help is generously recognized in the papers, either by getting the sports editor to put in a comment or by a letter to the editor from you and your committee.

Have a car follow the last-place walker. If you can get a police car to lead the first walker, that's nice, but asking for such a thing is a bit presumptuous if you have only a dozen or fewer walkers in the race.

Make sure that the paper cups and other debris along the course are cleaned up. Clean up the finish line area, too.

If you can get a school or other locker-room facility to use for dressing, that's fine, but if it means paying a janitor for several hours of his time, you would be better off asking the walkers to come dressed for competition. Then at the end when they will be coming in spread out over several minutes, you can invite them all to dress at your house before they start attacking the edibles.

Have the race results written large and clear as soon as possible after the race, and post a copy of these results where everyone can study them. Give out the prizes as soon as the last walker finishes. Some of your competitors may want to get home as soon as possible, so don't keep them waiting unnecessarily.

If the local newspapers aren't eager enough to send someone to the race, make a telephone call that same evening and pass along the results plus any interesting sidelights that have occurred. Most small-town papers will print things that are carefully fed to them, but often they lack the initiative or the manpower to go out and give live coverage.

If you do all your groundwork carefully, and if you are fortunate enough to get volunteers to time (two people), to drive the car following the race (one person), and to judge (one person), you can leave your four volunteers to do their jobs and you'll be free to compete in the race. As a competitor, you will be in a position to know just how successful your planning was. If you enjoy competing in the race, the chances are that all of the walkers are going to feel much the same way.

The most embarrassing thing that could happen would be that you would win your own race, thus prompting all sorts of jokes about the size of your ego and the like. But that's the sort of embarrassment that you're looking for when you start competitive walking. You'll thrive on it!

17

What Will Your Doctor Think?

For the answer to this question, I turned to a doctor who should know walking and walkers better than other medical people, George Lattarulo of Boston.

George is one of the most experienced racewalkers in America. Like me, George also enters running races as well as walks, but he does it on an amazing scale. In a typical year, he will enter roughly 200 races, perhaps 130 of them running, the other 70 walking. (He would enter more walks if they existed, but he settles for running races as the next best thing.)

He has eight New England walking championships to his credit, one national (100 kilometers in Colorado in 1975) and two more national gold medals for being a member of a championship team (the North Medford Club, of which I also am a member). His second-third-place medals are innumerable.

Three years ago in Columbia, Missouri, George became the thirtieth American to qualify as a Centurion. That means he covered 100 miles on a track (400 times around) in less than 24 hours. He played it close, taking 23 hours, 50 minutes, 37 seconds. Since then, nine others have become members of this select group, three of them women.

Thus, in Dr. George Lattarulo you have not only a man who knows about the theories of what the body can do, but also an athlete who has experienced more of what his own body can handle than most men will ever suspect.

To get the most valuable information possible from George, I asked my walking friends what they wished they knew about how the body works in their sport. I grouped the various questions into some semblance of order and wrote them down in a long letter to George. He went over the questions carefully, and in a couple of weeks he came up with what you will read in these pages.

As I said earlier, he tells a little more than I need to know in some instances, but for those who take a less casual attitude toward things than I do, the following answers with their twin bases of medical knowledge and common sense should put you on the right track as far as keeping your body in the best possible condition is concerned.

The first set of questions I asked were all about the feet and legs—the chief trouble spots for runners. Their condition is obviously of paramount concern to walkers as well. Here's how our question-answer exchange went:

Gray: Blisters are the one ailment that I have suffered from because of walking, so I thought I'd start right at the bottom of things and work up. How does one avoid blisters, and how does one treat them when the avoiding fails?

Lattarulo: Blisters are caused by ill-fitting or poorly constructed shoes or socks. The foot rubs repeatedly across an uneven part, and heat caused by friction develops the blister. Blisters should not keep you from walking. Cover small ones with first-aid cream, then tape them carefully.

Larger blisters, ones so big that they hurt, must be popped with a sterilized needle and kept clean as the major danger is infection. Do not cut the skin away. Squeeze out all the fluid, cover with a gauze pad, and tape. Usually you will be able to walk without pain after proper treatment of even a large blister. There is no need to consult a doctor unless infection develops.

Gray: Is a bone bruise as bad as it sounds? What's the best treatment?

Lattarulo: Bone bruises are not common among racewalkers as the distribution of weight is more uniform than in running. A bone bruise is merely an inflammation of the heel caused by repeated pounding. However, sufferers of Morton's foot, whose second toe is larger than the first, can experience trauma to the second metatarsal and hence pain in the ball of the foot. Padding placed behind the area of pain can ease the situation. In serious cases, orthotics may be called for.

Gray: What is plantar fasciitis?

Lattarulo: This is an inflammation at the point where the sole joins the heel. Excessive pronation and overuse can inflame the dense fibrous band that runs under the foot from the ball to the heel. The problem should not be neglected as heel spurs or calcium deposits can develop in the inflamed area. If rest and better shoes don't solve the problem, see an expert as prescribed exercises or orthotics are needed.

Gray: How about posterior tibial tendinitis?

Lattarulo: The tendon on the back of the leg muscle may tighten up in running, but in walking there is more even development of the front and back muscles of the leg so this condition will hardly ever occur.

Gray: Is numbness of the feet anything to worry about?

Lattarulo: Not really. Numbness of the feet is caused by pressure on superficial nerves and is really no problem.

Gray: My runner friends all seem to worry about their Achilles tendons. What about them?

Lattarulo: Achilles tendinitis is not common among racewalkers. Excessive hill running, running on the toes, and excessive pronation can inflame the thick tendon that connects the heel to the back of the calf muscle. If you do have Achilles problems as a walker, it's probably been caused by walking on uneven surfaces, or a sudden lowering of heel height can precipitate the problem. Also the back of the shoe may be too tight. Rest and walking on even surfaces should alleviate the problem.

Gray: Another problem I've had once or twice is shin splints.

Lattarulo: Shin splits also are inflamed tendons and muscles. Constant pounding causes weakening of the long arch of the foot. This leads to separation of the foot bones and widening of the foot. In domino fashion, ankle ligaments are stretched, and the lower leg muscles in resisting the stretch are torn away from the shin bone. You probably got your shin splints from running, and the answer to the problem is obviously to cut out the running part of your program until the shin splint pain goes away.

Gray: Because chrondomalacia patellae is called "runner's knee," I assume that walkers don't get it. Is this correct and why?

Lattarulo: You're right. Runner's knee is no problem in racewalking. When you have weak quadriceps in relation to the hamstring, there is an imbalanced pull at the knee cap. If the kneecap's alignment is incorrect, you get serious problems. All of this refers to running, not walking.

Gray: How about tightening of the hamstrings?

Lattarulo: Muscles in the back of a walker's leg are not as tight as among runners because there is more even development. Walking is a gliding motion while running is really a series of continuing jumps, putting as much as three times body weight on each leg. The muscles at the back of the legs overdevelop in running. In walking, the quadriceps in front develop as well as the hamstrings, and there is less tightening. This is one reason racewalkers have fewer back problems than most people, because there's a direct relation between tightening of the hamstrings and certain back problems.

Gray: What about cramps?

Lattarulo: Cramps may be caused by a chemical imbalance between acetylcholine, which causes the muscles to contract, and its neutralizer, cholinesterase, which relaxes the muscles. Cramps may also be caused as a result of a salt, potassium, magnesium, calcium, or vitamin B deficiency. Cramps can be relieved by stretching, kneading, and slowing down.

Gray: I hope that stress fracture is another problem that walkers seldom have to worry about.

Lattarulo: Stress fracture is not a problem in walking except for those who go great distances in stiff boots. Because of the gliding motion in racewalking, there ordinarily are no problems.

Gray: Everyone experiences some muscle soreness. Is there anything we should know about it?

Lattarulo: Muscle soreness is caused either by microscopic tears that will heal with one or two days of rest or by a build-up of waste products in the muscle. The latter condition can be lessened by warming down after a workout in much the same way you warm up at the start. You should also take a light workout on any day after a stressful one that leaves you with muscle soreness.

Gray: Is a side stitch anything to worry about?

Lattarulo: It's not dangerous, but it hurts. A stitch is a spasm of the diaphragm, which is the muscle that lies between the abdomen and the lungs. With better fitness and more relaxed breathing, the problem subsides. Also, operating on a full stomach can increase the athlete's susceptibility to stitches. If a stitch occurs during a race, slowing the pace and groaning may relieve the air pressure.

Gray: I have a friend who has had blood in his urine after running. I'd quit if that happened to me. How bad is it?

Lattarulo: It's not usually very bad. The most common cause of bloody urine is usually hemoglobinuria, which results from excessive destruction of red blood cells. Extreme exhaustion or an allergy may precipitate the problem. However, since kidney pathologies may cause similar symptoms, you should collect an immediate sample of the urine and bring it to the doctor.

Gray: Is any special diet necessary for the athlete in serious training? You know, vitamins, carbo loading, and things like that.

Lattarulo: Sound nutrition for athletes is sound human nutrition. So-called stress vitamins and special diets are bogus. Protein and vitamin requirements are practically the same for sedentary as for active persons. Obviously, there is a need for more calories in the more active. This caloric increase should be done by increasing carbohydrate intake. Cereals and grains are an excellent source.

Incidentally, in the short term, fad diets are probably not so bad; and in the long term, people can't stay with them anyway.

As for carbo loading, there was a study done in Sweden, but it was inconclusive. For one thing, the distance involved was a thirty-kilometer race, and there's really no extreme depletion of glycogen at that distance. The people who really did show improvement in the experiment were the more untrained athletes. As for the top performers today, I'm pretty sure that they don't carbo load. And most people don't follow it through correctly anyway. They eliminate the fasting or depletion part and just load up. And you have an increase in body weight because glycogen binds up water.

Gray: Of course, I know that alcohol, tobacco, and marijuana can't possibly help you, but how much can you use them without ill effects?

Lattarulo: With alcohol, moderation is the thing. It's only when the liver is overburdened that alcohol is a problem. The liver can metabolize a certain amount, depending on body size. Usually it's safe to take one drink an hour, two drinks per day. If you limit yourself to that, there is no ill effect in alcohol.

Smoking anything is another story. Smoking is a factor that has been associated directly and indirectly with a plethora of diseases. I don't know any top walker who uses marijuana—unless it's on the sly.

Gray: How long should you wait to train after eating?

Lattarulo: How long you should wait before training is very individual. Exercise does divert blood away from the digestive system, but you have to find out what suits your own system.

Gray: What should you drink during a race or workout and how much?

Lattarulo: You should certainly satisfy your thirst and probably drink as much as your stomach can handle. The commercial replacement drinks contain far too much salt and other things. As I said before concerning vitamins and protein, the requirements for an athlete are not substantially greater than for the sedentary person. In fact, salt depletion in an untrained person is greater initially, but with training, it is lessened. So water is the best and safest drink, and the amount taken depends on the individual.

Gray: What does walking do to make a healthy heart better?

Lattarulo: Walking has a training effect and strengthens the pumping action of the heart. It causes an increase in high-density lipoprotein (HDL), which clears the cholesterol from the tissue and brings it to the liver to be excreted. There is a direct correlation between your level of physical fitness and the lowering of things such as blood glucose, cholesterol, body weight, blood triglycerides, body fat, and blood pressure. Walking helps with all of these things.

Gray: What should the person with a bad heart do as far as walking is concerned?

Lattarulo: It all depends on what you mean by "bad heart." As long as the individual feels fine, he can do as much as he is capable of. You go by feeling in this matter. There are no rules that will fit every situation.

Gray: Somewhere I read that runners and walkers have "endurance hearts" that are different from those of other athletes. Is this true?

Lattarulo: That's not a very scientific term. Walking and running both have a direct effect on the development of the heart, so people in both sports do have stronger hearts than, say, football players. But the heart is the result of exercise; it's not that the so-called "endurance heart" was different to begin with.

Gray: How often should a racewalker have a complete physical examination?

Lattarulo: There's one line of thought that says that the annual physical checkup is an unnecessary ritual. Your body will put you on notice when something is amiss. Only your blood pressure needs checking. There are all kinds of sophisticated laboratory tests, but even when they reveal some irregularity, the problem usually has no treatment possible until you develop some symptoms. I'd say that if you have been training regularly and feel fine, then you don't need a physical.

Gray: What do you think of the pulse-taking method described in Chapter 5?

Lattarulo: Pulse taking is good for monitoring the efficiency of the heart. For determining the "good" workout, it's valid.

Gray: Do you approve of the hard-day–easy-day routine for the walker who wants to work out every day?

Lattarulo: It's not that simple. It all depends on the individual. The best general rule is that if you feel fatigue, don't work out until rested.

Gray: How much sleep is good for you, and what do you think of taking naps?

Lattarulo: Sleep is strictly an individual matter. Whatever you need is right for you. Naps are fine if you're accustomed to them, but if you're not, they can impinge on a good night's sleep.

Gray: Can you go into too many races? Or can you simply just train too hard?

Lattarulo: Both racing and training have the same rules. If you start feeling depressed, have trouble sleeping, suffer chronic muscle soreness, you're trying to do too much. Otherwise, you can race as much and train as hard as you have time for.

Gray: Is heat stroke the main danger in walking?

Lattarulo: Yes. Keep your head covered on hot days. Take plenty of water. Monitor your system carefully and use common sense.

Gray: When does cold weather get dangerous?

Lattarulo: It's the wind-chill factor, not the temperature, that you should watch. It's not harmful to breathe cold air. It's mere superstition that warns you of such dangers. But you have to be careful about clothing. You don't want to get hypothermia. Again, common sense is your answer to potential problems with cold weather.

Gray: Are there any special precautions or limitations for women during the menstrual period?

Lattarulo: No. No special precautions are needed.

Gray: Are there any special dangers or benefits to walking, serious walking, after menopause?

Lattarulo: There's no difference between men and women as far as walking during your later years is concerned. As you state in Chapter 21, increased fitness helps combat the various things that old age inevitably brings, but it is the same for both sexes. For example, osteoporosis begins when you are twenty-five or so. The bones start to lose calcium, and exercise does help the bones to lay down more calcium.

Gray: How do muscles get stronger? Will understanding the process help you to be a better walker?

Lattarulo: John, it would take me a whole chapter to outline that answer, and then you probably wouldn't understand half of it. Let's settle for saying that you wouldn't be any better a walker if you did understand the process. Otherwise, doctors would be world beaters.

Gray: Here's my final question. Does racewalking help you to live longer?

Lattarulo: There are no definitive studies on this question, but I believe that, yes, it will. There is no question that walking strengthens your heart and frees you from worry about heart trouble, so it stands to reason that if you're not going to die of a heart attack, then statistically your life should be a little longer. The main point I'd like to make, however, is that whether or not walking adds years to your life, it will make more enjoyable however many years you do have.

18

Does Walking Really Give You a Sound Mind?

If there is anything about running books that irks me (and there certainly is), it's the oft-repeated claim that running is akin to taking drugs, only safer. "Runner's high" is supposed to be a marvelous, other-worldly experience. Well, I've been high on a few things in my life, but I have never gone vertically on a run. Moving horizontally has always taken all of my concentration, and I've never gotten high on running.

Maybe I'm jealous because of my deprivation, but I am afraid that if you are going to decide your walking career on the answer to whether or not you get walker's high, the chances are that you're going to have a very short career. I have yet to find anyone who knows much about this so-called "high."

However, even though you may not get any fantastic spiritual experience out of your daily walk, you still will benefit mentally, I believe. Walking does help to keep the world in perspective. I always take a long workout when I am in any sort of distress. I've been doing

127

it for close to forty years, and it has never failed to help. I recommend the therapy of fast walking.

I must admit that on one desperate occasion, the workout backfired to a degree. At school that dark March day in 1950, I had been notified that I was not getting tenure. What a polite euphemism for being fired! It was my first job, and it was at a prestigious school. I was crushed.

My wife wasn't home to console me, so that afternoon I went out for a hard workout. Near the end when I was very tired and moving slowly, I came across the body of a man who had drowned himself just a few minutes earlier; his footprints still showed clearly in the light snow that was falling. Although I had been moving with difficulty up to the moment of my gruesome discovery, I suddenly was able to run like the wind with my terrible message that a man was drowned in the reservoir.

As you can imagine, that didn't brighten up my day, but in a way it certainly showed me that things can be a lot worse than finding yourself young and healthy and out of work. At least I was alive. And it is the feeling of being alive, of being in tune with one's body and with one's world, that makes walking a mentally uplifting experience.

You also find a special spirit of camaraderie among walkers. It's there among runners as well, but there are so many runners now that the feeling isn't quite as special as with the select group that walkers still form in most areas.

Another difference between the two sports is that running is sheer power and pounding up and down, hardly conducive to conversation, while walking done properly is so smooth and nearly effortless that you get to watch the world go by without blurring, and you feel more like talking than runners do.

I once walked with a hearty sixty-year-old man who talked nonstop for the thirteen miles I was able to stay with him. He recently had recovered from his bereavement over the death of his wife of many years, and he had found a new girlfriend. He had also found a book on sex and was amazed to learn that there were many more positions for the sex act than the one that he and his wife had used. He discussed the "headlights" of his new woman friend. "She's got great headlights, John," he said. "All my women always had headlights. Even the wife had good headlights."

His one worry in the new romance was that the woman might get pregnant. As she admitted to being fifty-six years old, I assured him that if she did conceive, there would be considerable consolation in knowing that the two of them would be making the *Guiness Book of World Records*.

No one claims that walking will automatically bestow remarkable mental powers on you. Besides the ancient romancer I just told you about, there was another walker in New England years ago who cheerfully admitted that he had periodic lapses when he would be locked up in a "crazy house." He also bragged that he had never worked a day in his life, at least not for pay, and that he could talk nonstop by the hour and never make a grammatical error. As an English teacher, I constantly (and unconsciously) monitor everything I hear or read. And Charley was correct; I never heard him speak a sentence that didn't parse perfectly.

Charley wasn't a great walker, but he was strong. He was the one who showed up for the annual twenty-kilometer race in Taunton having gotten up early that morning and walked over from Providence. In other words, he had warmed up for his twelve-mile race by strolling a leisurely twenty miles.

Robert was the leading dimwit among New England walkers. He was definitely a moron. Already well into his thirties, he still spoke of his plans to attend Brown University and to major in aviation—as soon as he managed to get his license to drive a car.

Ignorant, crazy, or just plain thick, they were all nice guys, all friends of the rest of the walkers in New England, and the rest of us were mostly an intelligent bunch, I modestly admit. We still were able to get along with the less gifted as friends. It's a good feeling to be a part of a group, and that is one of the mental strengths that walking brings you.

Walking also makes you appreciate nature more. When you are traveling 2,000 miles a year (that's only six miles a day, or a bit over an hour's effort), you see a lot of the world. Seeing the world makes you realize at once both your own insignificance and your own wonderful sharing in so much magnificence. You find so many old clichés coming marvelously into your own life, from "Oh, beautiful for spacious skies" down to the wondrous complexity of a blade of grass.

I have never read or heard of racewalking being used as therapy for the mentally disturbed, but I suspect that there must be a period in a person's recovery when walking would indeed help to keep the world in perspective. Certainly for the normal person, walking is a nearly ideal way to get your act back together. I know that I frequently was seriously worried about things involved with teaching.

(Don't let anyone tell you that teaching is anything but hard work.) Yet even on the worst days, once I arrived home, changed into my training clothes, and went out for a workout, I automatically felt better. When you are pushing your body, your mind doesn't have time to torture itself with unproductive worry.

At the same time, somewhat paradoxically, a long training walk is the best time for working out problems, for thinking of just what you are going to do in such and such a situation. Somehow the walking enables you to divide your thinking into two parts—the useless worrying and the constructive planning—and to discard the useless.

In fact, it's very much the opposite of what sometimes happens to me when I am trying to go to sleep at night. I'll start worrying about something that I have no control over. Soon the worry engulfs me; my stomach starts to churn; and the no-sleep-tonight signal flashes endlessly in my brain. I can't control my thoughts. I try to think of productive things, but the stupid worry creeps right back in and monopolizes my thoughts.

If you ever have had that experience at night, you owe it to yourself to try walking and see if the reverse holds true. I think you will find that a good long walk—real walking, not strolling—will clear your brain and set it to work in profitable ways.

My next claim for the psychological blessings of walking is much harder for me to pinpoint and will undoubtedly be hard for you to believe, but I'll tell you about it anyway, and as you become more and more involved with the sport, you can check me out and see if you agree.

This final argument in favor of long-distance racewalking is that walking makes you a nicer person. I've been walking for over thirty years, and while I have met all sorts of characters, brilliant and stupid, teetotalers and alcoholics, big men and scrawny women, all shapes, religions, and colors of humanity, I have never met a really nasty person. Somehow, hard training drives out that Mr. Hyde portion that resides deep down in the finest Dr. Jekylls.

Well, I told you that you would find it hard to believe, but it's been true for me, and I have read of and talked to others who feel the same. Long-distance walking somehow brings out the best in a person's character. Anyway, I told you you didn't have to believe me. Just get out and try the sport for a few years, meet all the other walkers in your part of the world, and decide for yourself.

Maybe you'll even turn into a nicer person yourself.

Whether or not you find that walking produces a personality improvement for you, you will definitely share in the other psychological benefits. The old *mens sana in corpore sano* is still a worthy goal, and walking can help you attain the *mens* part as well as the *corpore*.

19

Is Walking Just Another Fad?

I **believe that the** embarrassment factor is the chief drawback to the success of walking as a sport. I don't know why the various strokes in swimming, the obviously unnatural techniques of the various field events in track, and the athletic dance steps that each generation finds for itself are all considered graceful while racewalking techniques are an embarrassment, but that is certainly the way it is.

One way to help overcome that embarrassed feeling is to develop pride in the sport of walking. And one way to develop that pride is to become aware of the history of walking, a history that is richer by far than those of the glamor sports of today.

Sports as we think of them in America today started toward the end of the nineteenth century. Major league baseball goes back to 1876, college football to Princeton–Rutgers in 1869, the modern Olympics to 1896, and Wimbledon tennis to 1877. Walking, however, was a big money sport long before any of the others. Walking suffered a strange decline between the 1920s and the 1970s, but other than those fifty years of this century, walking has been a big-time sport for over two centuries.

Edward Payson Weston

I received my introduction to the history of walking in 1952 when I received the Edward Payson Weston trophy for winning a race in Providence, Rhode Island. I looked up Weston in books and learned that he was a walker whose career started before the Civil War and lasted until the 1920s. During his long career, he walked to wealth as well as to fame. He earned $10,000 in one race (Portland, Maine, to Chicago) in 1867. When he was seventy years old, he earned in one race twice what a major league baseball star could make in a whole season.

At the same time I was reading about Weston, I also was competing against Gardner Spooner of New Bedford, another walking octogenarian. Gardner was, of course, very slow when I knew him, but he was a delightful man and had had a marvelous career. He had been born with only one hand, the other arm ending just below the elbow. That had not stopped him from playing hockey or from bicycle racing in his youth. By the time I knew him, he was in his seventies, a retired milkman who ran the Boston Marathon and took part in walking races.

One day I happened to mention Weston to Gardner, and he told me that as a young man he had seen Weston come striding through New Bedford, and he and some other kids had walked along with him. "We had to run to keep up," the old man remembered. It was a thrill for me to realize that I was competing against someone who had walked with a man whose career had started in 1861. I liked that.

Weston's career started before walking reached its height of popularity in America; in fact, Weston himself was more responsible than any other individual for the rise of walking as a spectator (and gambling) sport. His first long walk was undertaken because he lost a bet. He had bet against Lincoln in the 1860 election, and the wager was that the loser had to walk from Boston to Washington for the inauguration.

Weston was twenty-two years old at the time, and he enjoyed the long walk so much that he took up walking quite seriously after that. He was a professional pedestrian, and six years after his first long walk (he arrived late for the inauguration, incidentally, but was seldom late again) Weston walked the 1,326 miles from Portland, Maine, to Chicago in thirty consecutive days (though never on a Sunday), winning $10,000.

He was a natty dresser and always looked the proper Victorian gentleman, complete with necktie and hat, as he walked those great distances. He considered himself a "propagandist for pedestrianism" and he was a successful one. He put on exhibitions all over the East Coast, and they were well attended.

Americans then as now were considered inferior to the English as walkers, but in 1876 Weston won the Astley belt, the symbol of world supremacy, along with a side bet of $2,500 by covering 550 miles in 142 hours. That's over ninety miles a day for six days and would still put Weston among the top finishers even against today's best walkers.

In 1876, he walked 1,000 miles in England and a total attendance of over 200,000 paid to see him do it. At another time, he put on a Temperance Walk in which he went 5,000 miles in 100 days, stopping, as he always did, to preach wherever he was on Sundays.

On his last trip to England, he covered 127 miles in twenty-four hours. Today American walkers have a Centurian Club for those who have covered 100 miles in a day. At latest count, it is still a very select group of a couple of dozen Americans.

In 1906 when he was sixty-seven, Weston covered 100 miles from Philadelphia to New York in six minutes less than twenty-four hours. At sixty-eight, forty years after his first such walk, he covered the Portland to Chicago route (nineteen miles longer this time) and did it twenty-nine hours faster than when he was young.

On his seventieth birthday, he went the 512 miles from San Francisco to Los Angeles in twelve days—actually eleven days, as he took Sunday off as usual. (The man was no saint, however; he eventually left his Sunday school teacher wife and lived for twenty-two years with another woman.)

Also during his seventieth year he went from New York to San Francisco in 105 days, disappointingly slow in his own eyes. The next year, he went coast to coast in a truly remarkable seventy-seven days, earning $6,000 for the feat.

At age seventy-four, he walked the 1,500 miles from New York to Minneapolis, and an estimated 300,000 turned out to see him. Many of these must have been members of Weston Walking Clubs, which sprang up all over America to promote the sport.

Weston was still walking, living in New York, when he was eighty-eight years old. Then one day a taxi struck him, and he died a lingering death two years later, never walking again.

Other Old-Time Walkers

Although Weston is the most famous American walker of all time, he was hardly unique in his devotion and success in walking. In England, the tradition of amazing walking feats (and huge bets) antedated Weston by almost a century. In 1809, a Captain Barclay (real name Allardice) walked 1,000 miles in 1,000 hours on a one-mile stretch at Newmarket. For forty-two days, the man would walk a mile, then eat or rest for the remainder of the hour, then walk another mile and so on. Thus, for forty-two days he could never sleep for more than forty-five minutes at a stretch. On this race 100,000 pounds were wagered, a simply unbelievable sum for those times.. Barclay ate twice a day. At 5 A.M. he had fowl, ale, tea, bread, and butter. At noon, he had beef steaks or chops. He lost thirty-two pounds in the forty-two days and certainly proved that modern nutritionists don't have all the answers about proper diet for long walks.

How much of the 100,000 pounds Barclay received, I haven't been able to learn, but it must have been a big chunk, because in an earlier race he had won a bet of 5,000 guineas when he covered ninety miles in less than twenty-four hours, doing it on a muddy stretch of the York to Hull road.

Even before Barclay, there were famous walkers in England. For example, Foster Powell, born in 1734, did some great things including covering fifty miles in seven hours once; and in 1773 he went 400 miles from London to New York and back in five days, eighteen hours, an average of seventy-two miles a day. All distances and times can be trusted too, because there was always heavy betting and the resulting witnesses were not likely to accept erroneous figures.

Barclay's 1,000 repetitions gimmick gained more and more popularity, and by the middle of the nineteenth century walkers were aiming at 1,000 miles in 1,000 consecutive half hours. In 1851 Richard Manks did it first and won big money for his followers William Gale then did 1,500 miles in 1,000 hours and also 4,000 quarter miles in 4,000 successive quarter hours. That meant over forty days with never a nap longer than twenty to twenty-five minutes. In 1815, George Wilson was arrested after 750 miles of a projected 1,000-mile walk. His crime? Causing too many people to gather around.

Famous Women Walkers

In our own century, there have been some amazing walks as well. And women have gotten into the act. Eleanora Sears, a Boston socialite, was a great walker. She covered 109 miles in twenty-four hours in 1912, and in 1925 she did the forty-seven miles from Providence to Boston in ten and a half hours. The next year, she covered the same distance in forty-five minutes less, and in 1928 she went from Newport to Boston in seventeen hours.

In 1916, a woman named Minnie Hill Wood walked from Washington, D.C., to San Francisco in 140 days, hardly in a class with Weston but still pretty impressive. In 1960, Dr. Barbara Moore went from San Francisco to New York in eighty-five days, three of which were spent in a hospital after she was hit by a car in Indiana. She was fifty-five years old at the time and bragged, "I expect to live to be 150." She missed by about eighty years, dying in 1977.

Modern Walkers

If you are wondering about the ultimate in walking, you have to turn to the modern walkers, no matter how great the men of the past were. For example, John Merrill at age thirty-four walked 7,000 miles around the coast of England in ten months. He carried fifty pounds of equipment, too.

John Lees, also of England, went from Los Angeles to New York—2,876 miles—in fifty-three days, twelve and a quarter hours. The London to Brighton record set in 1957 by Dan Thompson still stands: fifty-two and a half miles in seven hours, thirty-five minutes, a time most runners would be pleased with.

Racewalking has become important in Mexico in recent years, and Mexicans have their share of world records. In 1977, Daniel Bautista covered twenty kilometers in 1:23.32. A year later, Raul Gonzales did fifty kilometers in 3:52.23. Mexicans won both walks at the 1984 Olympic Games.

Hugh Nelson of Great Britain has the record for 100 miles on the track, set in 1960. It is seventeen hours, eighteen minutes, fifty-one seconds. In 1978, Derek Harrison, also of Great Britain, covered 219½ kilometers in twenty-four hours. That's roughly 140 miles.

From all of this you can see that walking has a glorious tradition, quite independent of and superior to that of running. Runners around the turn of the century were only minimally competent by today's standards. For example, the early Boston Marathons were sometimes won in times over three hours—two minutes a mile slower than today's marathons. The 1,500-meter time in the first Olympics in 1896 was 4:33:2 by Edwin Flack of Australia, a time that would be mediocre for a local high school meet today, almost a minute slower than what Olympians can now do.

Compare that difference to differences between old-time walking records and those of today, and you have a bit of an idea of how dedicated the walkers of one hundred years ago were.

Then as now, money made the difference. For example, Weston had commercial sponsors for his walks. On his walk to Minneapolis, one sponsor was the maker of Weston Heel and Toe Walking Socks. On his seventy-seven day cross-country walk when he was seventy-one years old, a millionare put up $500 a day for every day under ninety that Weston managed. It didn't seem like much of a financial risk as the old man had taken over one hundred days the year before, but this time the spur of money brought him home in seventy-seven days, and he was $6,000 richer.

Weston had other good reasons to be dedicated to walking. He gave up the sport in middle age, but when he was sixty he suffered terribly from arthritis. As he was fond of saying in lectures, "Walking is almost a sure cure for rheumatism. In 1898, I started walking. I was able to walk only one block, then two, then three." He worked his way up from this crippled state to thirty-four miles every day. "I left my rheumatism on the road, and it's there yet," he concluded triumphantly.

Few of you reading this are going to emulate Weston or the other all-time wonders, but from these few examples out of thousands of other possibilities you must have gotten the idea of the almost infinite possibilities in walking. And from these examples you can draw inspiration and go after some more modest goals of your own.

Also think of this: Assuming that many of you are like me and enjoy impressing your friends, even though you may never make it coast to coast and may never walk a marathon faster than most people can run one, you can still become a sort of local legend by casually mentioning at your next big card game or during a lull in the football talk, "Oh, yeah, I'm tired. I walked over to _____ (mention a place ten miles away) today, and I kind of feel it now."

Going from one place to another that takes anyone a good bit of time to reach in a car is the single quickest way to impress your friends.

Whether you keep your new sport a semi-secret, training only in lonely places, or flaunt your new hobby all over town is strictly up to you, and the differences in the basic and important things are trivial. The main thing that you are going to get out of taking up serious walking, training to make your body a better instrument and perhaps even graduating to the point where you enter walking races, is that you are going to feel better about yourself.

It is almost impossible to walk five fast miles and stay depressed. It is equally impossible to walk fast daily and not enjoy your sleep each night a bit more than you ever did. Your food will taste better. Your sex life almost certainly will improve, especially if you can get your partner to go out and walk with you. Your appearance will improve. Your self-image will blossom. You will feel good about yourself.

It is really nice to feel good about yourself. Walking can do a lot toward giving you that feeling.

Walking definitely is not just another fad.

20

Should Little Kids Take Up Walking?

I am opposed to organized athletics for little kids. There are national running records for two year olds, and I believe that's obscene. I hate to see Little League parents yelling at the children. Furthermore, adult organization seems to rob kids of the initiative to get out and play sandlot games. When I was a kid, we played baseball, football, or whatever practically every afternoon. Now it seems the kids only play when their parents set things up for them. Adult pressure on kids in sports is often a disaster. For example, as a track coach I picked up a retired tennis player who had already grown tired of his best sport by the time he had gotten good enough to be a ranked player among the twelve year olds. Things seem even worse for swimmers and gymnasts, most of whom seem to quit competition before they are old enough to vote.

How much should kids participate in walking? Anything they want to do is okay. Anything their parents push them into doing is suspect. (The one exception comes when parents insist that kids walk to get some place. Parents who chauffeur their kids to school, scout meetings, music lessons, and Little League games and practice are wrong. Make them walk—at least up to a mile or two.)

The only organized walking our kids ever did was our Great

Massachusetts Coast Walk. This was an idea my son and I had twenty years ago. We would walk the coastline of our state. Before we started, my youngest daughter, then eight, wanted to come along, friends of all three children joined in, and even my wife and a friend of hers became coast walkers. The impressive thing about it all for me was that Kate and her friends, ages eight to ten, proved capable of walking the twenty or so miles we had scheduled for each day. They not only finished, but they finished with plenty of pep to spare. Kids really can walk.

There are age-group competitions for kids as well as for aging adults, but I still believe the important thing is not to push your kids into competition. If you do, you may be defeating your own purposes. I will use myself as an example again. I was convinced that Linda, my older daughter, could be a good walker. I used all my persuasive powers to get her and a couple of friends into some women's walking races back in the mid-sixties. Linda did fairly well, but she also learned to dislike competition. She seldom walks in races today.

On the other hand, Kate went into those early races against my better judgment. She was only eight or nine and much too young to compete, I thought. I never encouraged her. Then when she was in high school, I was the cross-country coach, and even though I had a girls' team I never pressured Kate to take part in the races.

Unlike Linda, Kate today is quite a competitor, consistently finishing in the top three in women's running races on Cape Cod and actually making it to the top six in competition against men in New England championship races in walking.

So let your kids alone; encourage them to take nice walks with you—almost all children like them—but don't try to live your athletic life through the exploits of your children. (Those who live on their kids' exploits are often exploiting them.)

If your child wants to compete, however, you don't have to worry about the ill effects of walking. There is some medical dispute about the effect of running on a youngster's growth. All that pounding may have an adverse effect. There is none of that, however, in walking. And since Dr. George Sheehan has called the typical nine-year-old child "pound for pound the world's best endurance athlete," you can take your kid on long walks and your only worries will be about your own survival, not the child's.

Children are divided by our schools and the peripheral after-school sports programs into two sharply divided groups: the Haves and the Have-nots. The Haves are the starting players on the school's sports teams, the same kids dominating all three seasons from September to June. That is, the star scorer in field hockey and the quarterback in football will be the kid who brings the ball up court in basketball and either pitches or plays shortstop in the spring.

The Have-nots are neglected. They may get a few calisthenics and have twenty minutes twice a week to play some innocuous game on the school playground (and even those games will be dominated by the Haves), but the Have-nots won't get much exercise.

The more walking you can get these Have-not kids to do, the better. Instead of volunteering to manage a Little League team the way jock parents do, why not simply take some kids for a hike on Saturday? You don't have to heel and toe at ten-minute miles. Your own schedule should include days of LSD (long, slow distance), and you can take some pretty remarkable walks with a group of kids, all of you enjoying and benefiting from them.

When I was a young man, I used to belong to an informal walking club. About half a dozen of us would meet at a house and walk from there to a barroom somewhere. We would rest, drink a beer, and then head back to the starting point, trying to follow a different route. It was fun, and we put in quite a few miles, averaging five or six miles each outing. You can do the same with the kids, substituting an ice-cream parlor for a barroom as your goal.

Even though I have specifically stated that I hope you don't enter your children in walking races, I do feel that you should teach them the racewalking style. If this style is learned when the child is young, it can actually help the child's physical development for life. Many of the back, foot, and leg problems that haunt American society would disappear if everyone walked properly. You don't have to compete in a championship race to benefit from the improved posture, coordination, and gracefulness that racewalking style can bring to a young person's life. Unlike the skills of football, ice or field hockey, and basketball, the skills of walking are good for a whole lifetime.

Give your children and their friends the fundamentals of racewalking. Don't try to overcoach them, and don't get excited when one of them proves to be extremely good at the sport. Don't rush the child into competition in the next race you go to. Sure, the race may have special age-group prizes for kids, but don't let your ego tell your child what to do.

Here's my suggestion: Take the children with you to a race. If they see other kids competing and feel cheated, or if they beg to be permitted to race in the next competition, let them. Just don't push them.

Of course, I'm talking about big-time races. Any time you want to arrange an impromptu race around the block, down the beach, or whatever, go ahead. Children love competition, and it never hurts them as long as the pressure isn't too great. If you yourself have developed a casual, enjoy-yourself attitude that this book promotes, that attitude will prove contagious, and your children will have fun from competition without any attendant misery when they lose.

There is one exception to my don't-push rule. If you know a child who has been brutalized by the physical education system to the point where his or her self-esteem is dragging, consider the psychological rewards of having that child go into a race and win a medal. Such children have always been chosen last for every sport, the typical right fielders who are usually small, always awkward, always searching for success and seldom finding it. They retreat to books (if they are lucky) and to television (if they're part of the huge majority).

To encourage one of these self-styled losers to walk is a real service to the child's future. Don't expect these children to be instant successes at walking, however. They will probably get their prizes by coming in third out of three when there are three prizes offered, but back home the other kids are going to see only the trophy or the medal, and the child that was being patterned for life-long losing suddenly has the respect of even the biggest jocks in the class.

Indeed, walking is a fine sport for kids as well as for adults. You can encourage them to walk all they can, and you never have to worry about hurting them physically.

It's the psychological damage of pushing children into competition too soon that I'm warning against. If your child goes into competition, don't get excited. One of the most repulsive sights in the world for me is the parent-turned-maniac at youth sports events. It's bad enough at Fenway Park or Madison Square Garden, but at least the objects of love and hate in those cases are professional athletes, well paid for the abuse they take.

To see children alternately idolized and berated for the way they perform and to see the adult world put pressure on young athletes seems wrong to me. Take your children's successes casually, laugh off their failures.

There's an old cliché: Show me a good loser, and I'll show you a loser. But what's so bad about losing? If there are ten people competing, nine of them are going to be losers. The important thing is that they be good losers.

On the other hand, if there are ten people competing, nine of them are also winners, compared to the ones behind them. When I finish 300th in a field of 700, I figure that I've chalked up 400 victories in that race. It's a philosophy that makes sports much more enjoyable, and it certainly keeps off the pressure. Try it with your children. And with yourself!

21

What About the Older Walker?

In 1955, when I was thirty years old, I sold an article about marathons to the *Saturday Evening Post* entitled "I Love to Run and Run and Run." In it, I happened to mention that I intended to go on racing until I was forty, which at that time seemed pretty old. Well, I'm over sixty now, and I still like to run, although as I have mentioned several times already, it doesn't compare to walking for reliable pleasure. I am wiser now as well as older, and I know that I am going to keep on racing for as long as I can. And the odds are that I can racewalk for years longer than I can run.

Very few things are different for the older walker from what is true for the younger one. I guess the biggest difference is that it takes an old body longer to recover from an injury. That in itself is a great argument in favor of walking as the best exercise for the older athlete. It's injury-free.

The worst excuse in the world for anything and an excuse that is used all too often is, "I'm too old for that." I hope you never use it. When I was a young man, I worked at various summer jobs to supplement my teacher's pay. One summer I used to eat lunch with my fellow workers in a park, and there was an old man, over eighty, who used to drop around a couple of times a week to sit and chat with us.

He was funny, full of good stories, and a pleasant companion. We were always glad to see him.

About once a month he would approach us with a little extra spring in his step, and we knew what he was going to say. As he drew near the group, he would announce, "Heh, heh, fellahs, I got in the saddle again last night." His wife, whom we never met, was over eighty too. I remember that old man and his announcements because it gave—and gives—me hope for a long future for myself. That old couple didn't moan "We're too old for that." I'm sure their lives were better because they didn't.

So don't give up on yourself just because you're old. Follow a few basic rules, and you can do some amazing things regardless of age.

Age-Group Competition

Not only are you never too old to exercise, but you also are never too old to compete. Age-group competition has long been an important part of tennis and golf. Now it's there for walkers as well. Almost all races have a master's division for those over forty, and the better races have divisions for over fifties and over sixties as well.

In national competition, there are age divisions every five years—or there should be. I remember the 1977 national masters' track meet in White Plains, New York. I was calmly resting between my two events, the three-mile walk and the two-mile run, and I was lying on a jumping pit. Two very old men were sitting at the other end, and I eavesdropped on their conversation.

One of the men was really upset. "How can they have us in ten-year groups at a national?" he asked. "Up in Toronto next month it will be five-year groups. That's the way it should be. How am I supposed to compete against youngsters only seventy and seventy-one? I don't have a chance."

He wasn't being funny. At seventy-eight, he saw "only seventy" as very young.

You are as young as you feel. Sure, it's a cliché, but clichés come into existence because they are true. If you start walking seriously, you will indeed feel young, and in a sense you will be young.

I'll use myself as an example. I have arthritic tendencies, and in the early morning I hobble around looking my age and a bit more, but I loosen up as the day progresses. By the time my tennis match rolls around, I'm ready to play on fairly equal terms with rivals less than half my age.

In running races, I now set a goal of beating over half the other runners. If there are 700 runners as there were in my last race on Cape Cod, I aim at beating 350 or better. (I came in 331 in this race, so it was a good one for me.)

I see no reason why I can't continue that for quite a few years. Johnny Kelley is in his late seventies, seventeen years older than I, and he still beats me fairly regularly in races, just as he defeats runners who are less than a third his age.

I am a better walker than I am a runner, and I aim higher in walking races. In New England races, I want to be in the top six because there are six championship medals in each race. I still manage to do that occasionally.

So I hope I've made my point that you don't need to sit around and rest just because you're "old." "Rest" and "rust" are very close to the same word. You don't want to rust out, do you?

You will find living examples of older athletes who have continued to excel in spite of advancing years anywhere that walkers gather. My friend Tony Medeiros is one fine example. A top-ten finisher in the Boston Marathon when he was younger, Tony switched to walking as he grew older, and he did some amazing things. Perhaps his most amazing accomplishment was one year in the forty-kilometer national championship at Long Branch, New Jersey, one of the oldest and best races in the country. Tony came back with the gold medal for first walker over sixty. He was also the first man over fifty. For that matter, he was the first one over forty, and he was twelfth overall in a race in which the top finishers were Olympic team candidates.

About the only thing you can't do when you are old is beat the younger athlete who puts in equal time and dedication to the sport. There is more zip and spring in the young legs, and in a showdown the good twenty-five year old is going to beat the good fifty-five year old. The other side of the record, however, is that the really good fifty-five year old will beat all those ordinary twenty-five year olds, and there are always many more ordinary competitors than extraordinary ones in a race.

So don't be afraid to compete.

The Benefits

Conversely, don't feel you have to compete. Even though I have been emphasizing competition, the most important benefit from walking for the older person is the feeling of health and well-being. Those feelings certainly do not automatically come to the older citizen. The magic strength and joy of living that the young enjoy become more and more rare as the body ages. There are new aches and pains, new sniffles, new blotches, and all the old woes intensify. Walking can't halt old age, but it certainly can put it in remission. You never beat Old Man Time, but you can delay the ultimate victories of that old tyrant, and that's what this chapter is all about.

If I haven't been very specific yet, that's because the main problem is a psychological one. If I can't persuade you to get out there and try to walk fast, it doesn't much matter what else I say. If you never work out, then zero times anything is still zero.

According to a survey of Americans over sixty, only about four out of ten exercise regularly. About half of that forty percent choose walking as their favorite exercise. That's fine, except that the walking many of them do is of the 200-calorie-an-hour variety. I would like to see you double or triple that caloric effort, because you will be doubling and tripling the benefits without spending any more time doing it.

For the six out of ten of those over sixty who get no regular exercise, I say get out and start walking. You're already doing a good bit of it around the house even if it's only to go from the TV to the refrigerator. You know that you can make it from your front door to the first telephone pole and back. The next time, go two poles, three the third day, and so on. In a very few weeks, that simple method will have you covering sufficient distance to satisfy any body's needs. Then you can work on speed.

Actually, very few of you are in such bad shape that one telephone pole away will be far enough to turn you back. Most of you can make it all the way around the block. The next time, go a bit more than one block. And so on.

Most Americans already know that the best forms of exercise are those that strengthen the heart and improve the circulation— things like walking, running, and swimming, not things like golf and bowling. The curious thing is that older Americans know far less about this than younger age groups. If you are reading this and know of an older person who would benefit from more exercise, try to turn him or her on to walking. Plenty of people make it their business to turn others on to harmful drugs, so why shouldn't the rest of us counterattack a little and turn people on to a kind of kick that only can benefit them?

Attitudes

There are certain attitudes that older people are going to have to get rid of if they are to become successful walkers. For example, they must give up the somewhat wishful thinking that the need for exercise diminishes, even disappears, as they grow older. They must realize that the real health risk is not in exercising too vigorously but in not exercising enough. They must realize how much potential they still possess and that that potential is not going to be developed unless they follow a program of regular, planned exercise.

The feats of various older athletes have long since proved that the older athletes can be good ones. It is mostly a matter of getting the individual to realize that he or she can do something in the way of athletics. Walking is an obvious way toward gaining this realization. Swimming, bicycling, running, and the rest of the aerobic exercises all pose certain hurdles for the beginner who is both unskilled and old. Walking, however, can be done in gradual degrees. On your first outing, you may go a half a mile, let's say, and take almost fifteen minutes to do that.

Well, a thirty-minute-mile pace is not going to get you far in a race, but neither is it going to make a spectacle of you; you will look like exactly what you are—a person taking a little stroll. The equivalent from swimming or bicycling or running would be far more likely to make you look foolish. Interestingly enough, you don't have to worry about looking foolish in walking until you get quite good, quite fast, and your arms are pumping furiously while your rear end does its hip girdle bit. That's when you get the comments. By that time, however, you are so proud of yourself that a few rude remarks from the sidelines sound more like respect than like raspberries.

Special Problems

The special problems of the aging walker are in the loss of flexibility. The joints, tendons, and ligaments move less freely and are less elastic. The bones become more brittle and break more easily. The muscles lose some of their strength. None of that sounds good; all of it is inevitable to a degree. But "to a degree" is the key phrase. With proper exercise all of those losses due to age can be minimized. Whatever your age, you can become more fit.

Once you have been convinced that walking is the activity for you, the next thing to watch out for is overenthusiasm. If you have been sedentary for years, you have to ease into your new program of exercise. Walking is the easiest to ease into, but even with walking the overeager participant can hurt himself right at the start (men are the offenders in this regard more than women). Older walkers have to develop more slowly for two reasons. First, their patterns are so deeply established that any change, like a new style of walking, is going to be difficult. Second, using an old muscle in a new way leads to considerable risk of stiffness and pain the next day.

I recently became aware of both of these things at a tennis match. A friend of mine, in her sixties I think, was leaving Cape Cod to go home to Ohio, and she came to me for a lesson in walking, the lesson we had never gotten around to that summer. I stopped watching the match and went over to a driveway where I tried to tell her everything about walking in one fast lesson. I showed her the arm action, the hip girdle, the feet in a straight line, the stretching of the stride, and everything I could think of. She was so awkward that she looked more like a pretzel than a walker. Normally an attractive woman with excellent posture, she kind of turned herself into a caricature of Groucho Marx. Her husband, watching in mild amusement, eventually commented that if she went out on the streets of Bowling Green and walked like that, he would disown her.

Eventually the couple left, and another spectator came up to me and said that he had tried racewalking that summer himself. His granddaughter, visiting from Washington, was among the top walkers in the state, and she had given him a lesson. Now, Walter is somewhere around seventy and very athletic, playing good tennis and tending a few lobster pots off shore as a hobby. But he said to me, "John, after I tried that stuff, I couldn't move the next day. I was crippled."

Let those two friends of mine be a lesson to you. If you are old, don't try to do too much with technique too fast, and when you do try something new, don't go at it as a young athlete would. Take it easy and build up gradually. If you do go gradually, all should go well. As has been stated already many times in this book, racewalking is the ideal sport because it eliminates the stress and jarring of even the slowest jogging. As you get in shape to walk faster, your technique will improve and you will become smoother in your form, meaning that there will be less and less shock to your system. If you take things one step at a time and think in terms of improving over a year's time instead of a week's, then racewalking can be done at practically no risk of injury.

If you haven't had a good physical examination recently, be sure to have one before you try anything new in the way of exercise. Then always monitor your system as you walk along. Your body will let you know when you're trying too much too soon. A pounding in your heart, a pain in the chest, breathlessness, nausea, headaches, and trembling are all signs that should be heeded. Slow down or stop when you get any of these symptoms. If they persist, go back to your doctor and have him check them out.

Modifying the Training Charts

On the training charts (Chapter 8), you should take twice as long as suggested. That is, remain at the same level through two days or two weeks instead of one day or one week as outlined for the younger athlete. One of the things we all learn with age is patience, and you won't need to rush on to further improvement the way a younger person might. You know that there will always be time for better performances tomorrow.

Also, after you reach a certain level of fitness, don't get discouraged when you find it impossible to improve any more. Remember that at an advanced age merely holding even is sometimes quite an accomplishment. In age-group competition, for example, a time that would win the over-sixty championship might be back in the middle of the pack in the over-fifty division.

No one is going to find the Fountain of Youth, but walking will prove to be the best substitute you can find—not magic, but still somehow magical.

22

Final Words

Throughout these pages I have tried to explain why walking is such an amazingly satisfying form of exercise. In the third of a century that I've been a walker, I have gained numerous benefits, all of which I have already shared with you.

The best part of walking is that in spite of being over sixty, antique by most athletic standards, I not only see hope for the future but an actual likelihood that however many more years I may be allotted, these years will be among the best of my entire walking career.

The reason is not that I'm likely to become magically youthful but that I'm going to have so much more company in my walking. For years I was the oddball in town, the guy with the weird walk that you saw everywhere at all hours. No one ridiculed me—at least not to my face—but no one came out to join me either. Now all that's changing. People are starting to take up racewalking, and because of the snowball effect their numbers are going to grow ever more rapidly. It's going to be fun to have company on my long walks.

I once walked a mile in 7:19. Another time I covered sixty miles in a day—or rather thirteen hours of a day, after which I called up my niece for a ride the last ten miles of the seventy that I had planned on covering. The 7:19 mile earned me a second-place medal in a New England championship race, and I'll never manage that again, but the sixty miles was done just as a lark, to get me from Cape Cod to a visit with my mother and my niece. I know that some day I'm going to try that again and make it the full seventy miles next time.

If I am able to have these hopes and plans for the future after all the years that I have lived and walked, a beginning walker should be able to look forward to many times my future enjoyment.

The key to this enjoyment, however, is to take things casually. So much grimness has settled down like a vast fog over the land of runners that I worry about the same thing happening to walkers when they too proliferate. Runners used to be simple people who put on their old clothes and their comfortable shoes and went out for a run. For fun. Today the cheerful men and the merry women are greatly outnumbered by the "serious" runners who analyze and worry about every aspect of their sport.

I think it's marvelous that the top men and women runners can now make a good living from running, and I don't blame them a bit for being serious. But to see them slavishly imitated by the thousands of ordinary runners who take their sport about as humorously as a priest at the altar is something that makes me sad.

I blame the decline in runners' pure joy on commercialism. The fast-buck artists are on to exercise in a big way. Right now, they aren't too interested in walking because the sport is a minor one and so simple that there aren't many obvious ways of fooling people into parting with their money.

That's going to change, however. Walkers are increasing numerically in a way that's going to surprise everyone and that will make walkers fair game for the money grabbers. When that happens you're going to find all sorts of people who will try to separate you from your money. In so doing, they will also separate you from the simplicity that is the key to the pleasure of your sport.

Anything that detracts from your enjoyment of walking is a mistake. Never let any expert, book, or magazine article force you to do something that doesn't work for you.

Don't get so hooked on the fitness side of walking that you lose the fun part of it. Enjoyment comes first. If you don't enjoy, you won't continue.

Develop an attitude for yourself. Be your own coach. Make your own decisions. Listen to everyone (as long as the advice is free), but keep yourself as the one in charge. You'll have so much more fun that way—at least I have.

I have a warm feeling that walkers will always include a higher percentage of happy hoofers than runners now do. The reason for that is partly because there's no Boston Marathon in walking to overglamorize the sport. The ten-mile walk at Coney Island on Thanksgiving weekend is the oldest walking tradition in this country, and most people have never heard of the race, much less wanted to dedicate their year of training toward entering it.

More than that, the guarantee of happiness in walking lies in the fact that walking makes such good sense as a sport. I can't imagine people ruining it by turning it into an endless scientific seminar of physiology, psychology, and just about any other science you can think of, as runners have done. Walkers will always be doing something that they can enjoy, and as long as they keep their enjoyment in the foreground of their thinking, the sport is going to be a pleasure to them.

Let the masochists look elsewhere. Walking is fun. That it brings myriad benefits is merely a bonus, not its basic reason.

If you follow my suggestions, you'll be well on your way to a lifetime career as a walker. If you can automatically include one challenge as a part of everything you do, you can just about guarantee yourself success. That one challenge is a question: Am I enjoying myself?

If the answer is no, switch activities. Walking should be practically sybaritic. Now, sybarites are supposed to be old fatties, lying around in luxury, gorging on rich food and drink. Walkers are lean and hardworking. Yet if you have ever noticed how dogs love to take a walk, you have some idea of the natural pleasure involved in the act. Or if you have ever noticed how those happiest of humans, little children, love to keep on the move, how little they like to lie around doing nothing, you're beginning to realize the natural enjoyment to be found in physical activity, and suddenly my use of "sybaritic" in connection with walking doesn't seem so farfetched. My contention is that of all physical activities, you will find walking the most enjoyable.

Well, second most.

Walking is fun. May you enjoy yourself the rest of your days.

Racewalking Glossary

Achilles—the long tendon connecting the heel bone to the calf and an area of frequent injury for runners, seldom for walkers.

Age-group—competition in various races within races according to age. Standard groupings are junior (19 and under), open (20 to 39), submaster (30 to 39), master (40 and up), senior (50 to 59), grand master (60 and up). Age-group competition in national and international meets is sometimes further subdivided into five-year categories (40 to 44, 45 to 49, 50 to 54, and so on).

Bent knee—an illegal form of walking that will get you a warning.

Burst—a sudden increase in your pace during a race or training, so fast that it can be maintained only for a short distance.

Carbo loading—carbohydrate intake that supposedly increases one's staying power during a long race. It means eating mostly high-energy starch and sugar foods the last few days before an important race.

Centurian—a racewalker who has covered 100 miles or more on a track during a 24-hour period. A rare species.

Certified—a race course that has been measured according to TAC rules.

Creeping—an illegal way of walking with the knees failing to lock properly on each stride. Officially, the word is no longer used in racewalking. The illegality is now called "bent knee," a more easily understood term.

DNF—in race results, it means "Did not finish."

DQ—in race results, it means "Disqualified."

Endurance heart—a somewhat meaningless term that refers to the fact that racewalkers develop hearts that have greater endurance than they would otherwise have had. Endurance hearts are made, not born.

Fartlek—a Swedish word meaning "speed play" used to describe a training technique in which the walker goes at varying speeds in a free-form change of pace during the course of a workout.

Foot plant—the way a racewalker's foot hits the ground. The proper foot plant is to touch the ground with the heel first and then move along on the outside of the foot and push off with the toes.

Form—the way a walker moves. Also called "style" or "technique."

Hamstring—the big muscles at the back of the leg from the knee to the buttocks. Another area of injury for the runner but not usually for the walker because of the balance between pushing and pulling in racewalking.

Heavyhands—an exercise system invented by Dr. Leonard Schwartz designed to build a strong body by walking, running, and exercising with weights in one's hands.

Hip girdle—the key to walking technique. The hip is thrust down and forward to give the racewalker the maximum possible stride length.

In-form—walking at a slow pace concentrating on correct style and technique.

Intervals—a training technique in which short bursts of fast walking are alternated with recovery walks at much slower speeds. A typical interval workout might call for ten quarter miles at a fast pace with ten in-form quarters to rest in between.

Junior—an age-group category including all racewalkers nineteen years old or younger.

K—abbreviation for kilometer.

Kick—the final fast sprint at the end of a race, a dangerous time in racewalking because a competitor can be disqualified in the final quarter mile without a warning.

Lifting—losing contact with the ground; along with creeping, one of the two most common reasons for disqualification in a race. Also like creeping, the term is no longer used officially. "Loss of contact" is now the preferred term.

Locked knee—the position of the knee when the leg is properly straightened. You can feel the reason that it is called "locked" if you straighten your leg and concentrate on what the knee does. It is the most injury-free position that the knee can have when the foot strikes the ground.

LSD—Long, Slow Distance. Some wit long ago said, "I'm on LSD," describing his training, and the term caught on. It has nothing to do with drugs.

Masters—all racewalkers who are forty and over.

Open competition—races in which there is no age-group restriction or nationality requirement. It can also refer to the 20 to 39 year olds in age-group competition.

Overdistance—training at distances longer than the next race that you plan to enter.

Oxygen debt—the condition of needing more oxygen than your body can take in at the moment. You get out of debt by slowing down.

Pace—the speed at which you're walking. A ten-minute pace refers to miles run at an average speed of ten minutes. A two-minute pace interval session means one in which each quarter mile takes two minutes.

Patella groove—where the kneecap is when the knee is locked; the perfect position for avoiding knee injuries.

PR—Personal Record. The main goal of every racewalker, doing better in a race or over a training course than you have ever done before.

Pulled muscle—an injury in which the muscle fiber is torn.

Quadriceps—the large muscle in the front of the thigh.

Racewalking—a progression of steps so taken that unbroken contact with the ground is maintained.

Recovery period—in interval training the in-form walks between the all-out fast intervals.

Sanction—official approval from one of racewalking's governing bodies to conduct a race. Most walks have TAC approval.

Senior—an age category for racewalkers over fifty years.

Splits—times for fractions of a race, usually at the mile marks or every five kilometers.

Stitch—a pain in the side occurring when racewalking fast. This is a common thing with novice walkers but seldom occurs after one gets into reasonably good shape.

Stress fracture—a hairline break in a bone. It usually occurs from the stress of running, not from an accident, and it is a rarity in walking.

Street walking—normal walking with little or no hip girdle.

Stroll—an easy walk, either a street walk or an in-form racewalk style but one in which the walker pays no attention to style and simply enjoys the outing.

Support phase—that part of the two-stride walking cycle in which the body passes over the leg, and the full weight is on that leg.

Swing leg—either leg in racewalking when it is off the ground.

TAC—The Athletics Congress. The governing body for racewalking in the USA.

TSC—Two-Stride Cycle. The basis of all study of racewalking style, covering exactly what both legs do in both the support and swing phases of racewalking style.

Veteran—the English equivalent of "master" for walkers age forty and over in age-group competition.

Wall—the invisible object that rises up and strikes racewalkers when they are exhausted and unable to maintain their pace or form.

Walker's high—the near-religious feeling of wonder and euphoria that is supposed to be the ultimate reward of racewalking. Possibly a purely mythical thing.

Warmup and cooldown—everyone knows what a warmup is, but not everyone realizes that a cooldown period is equally important in avoiding injury, colds, and other ailments. Both involve a gradual change from the fast pace of a race or a hard training walk to the ordinary walk of everyday life.

Weight training—lifting various pieces of equipment according to various rules. Unnecessary for racewalkers who are willing to settle for overall fitness rather than aim at superhuman strength. (Weight training is also one way to step up one's overall fitness for those who are determined to be champions rather than settling for just being pretty good.)

Weight walking—a less rigorous, more pleasant way of developing upper-body strength for those who lack the self-discipline for a full Heavyhands program.

Rule 150— TAC General Rules of Racewalking

1. DEFINITION OF RACEWALKING. Racewalking is a progression of steps so taken that unbroken contact with the ground is maintained.

(a) During the period of each step, the advancing foot of the walker must make contact with the ground before the rear foot leaves the ground.

(b) The supporting leg must be straightened (i.e., not bent at the knee) for at least one moment when in the vertical upright position.

(c) Failure to adhere to the above definition of racewalking will result in disqualification. (See Rule 39.)

2. RACE CONDUCT. For all racewalking events, the following code of conduct must be adhered to, else disqualification will ensue:

(a) In track races a competitor who is disqualified must immediately leave the track, and in road races the disqualified competitor must, immediately after being disqualified, re-move the distinguishing numbers which he or she is wear-ing, and leave the course.

(b) In road races, a competitor may leave the road with the permission and under the control of a judge, provided that by going off the course the walker does not lessen the dis-tance to be covered.

3. SPONGING AND REFRESHMENT STATIONS.

(a) Sponging and Drinking Water Stations: At all walking events of 10 kilometers or more, sponging and drinking water stations may be provided by the Meet Director, Spon-sor or Organizers at suitable intervals, corresponding to weather conditions.

(b) Refreshment/Feeding Stations: In all races of more than 20 kilometers, refreshments shall be provided by the Meet Director, Sponsor or Organizers, and refreshment stations shall be arranged at approximately 5 kilometers and there-after at every 5 kilometers. Refreshments, which may either be provided by the organizer or the athlete, shall be availa-ble at the station assigned to the competitor. The refresh-ments shall be placed in such a manner that they are easily accessible for the competitors or so that they may be put into the hands of the competitors. A competitor taking refresh-ments at a place other than the assigned refreshment sta-tion may be disqualified.

4. COURSES AND CONDITIONS FOR WALKING EVENTS.

(a) In Championships, the circuit for the 20-kilometer walk should be, if possible, a maximum of 2,500 meters, and the circuit for the 50-kilometer walk should be, if possible, 2,500 meters, with a maximum of 5,000 meters.

(b) The organizers of walking events held on the roads must take care to ensure the safety of the competitors. In the case of Championships, the organizers must, where possible, give assurance that the roads used for the competitions will be closed in both directions; that is not open to motorized traffic.

(c) The road walking events shall be so arranged as to ensure that the walkers finish in daylight.

(d) The course for all Championship events and qualifying races must be certified according to Rule 133.

Rule 39— Judges of Racewalking

1. JUDGING.

(a) The Judges of Racewalking shall have the sole authority to determine the fairness or unfairness of walking, and their rulings thereon shall be final and without appeal. Judging decisions are made as seen by the human eye.

(b) The appointed Judges of Racewalking shall elect a Chief Judge.

(c) The Chief Judge shall assign the judges to the respective judging areas and explain the judging procedure to be used during the race.

(d) All the Judges shall act in an individual capacity.

2. WARNING.

Competitors must be warned by any judge when, by their mode of progression, they are in danger of ceasing to comply with the definition of racewalking (see Rule 150); but they are not entitled to a second warning from the same judge for the same offense. Having warned a competitor, the judge must inform the Chief Judge of his or her action.

3. DISQUALIFICATION.

(a) When, in the opinion of three Judges, a competitor's mode of progression fails to comply with the definition of racewalking (see Rule 150) during any part of the competition, the competitor shall be disqualified and informed of the disqualification by the Chief Judge.

(b) Disqualification may be given immediately after the competitor has finished, if it is impractical to inform the competitor of the disqualifications during the race.

(c) It is recommended that a system of signalling "warning" by a white flag and "disqualification" by a red flag be used as far as possible during a walking race for the information of the officials, competitors and spectators. Each Judge may also use a paddle or disc with the symbol ∿ indicating "Loss of Contact" and the symbol > indicating "Bent Knee" on reverse sides to show the reason for the warning or disqualification call.

TAC/USA
Association
Addresses

Many of the fifty-nine TAC associations cover a single state. Others are part of a state or cover more than one state. Wherever an association does not coincide with a state, a brief description is given.

Adirondack (northeast New York State)—726 Columbia Turnpike, East Greenbush, NY 12061

Alaska—Box 101611, Anchorage, AK 99510

Arizona—1735 W. Missouri Ave., No. 611, Phoenix, AZ 85032

Arkansas—1008 S. Cumberland, Little Rock, AR 72202

Border (the westernmost part of Texas around El Paso along the Mexican border)—6848 Pino Real, El Paso, TX 79904

Central (most of Illinois except the southern tip)—Box 457, Sterling, IL 61018

Colorado—5011 Bonita Way, Colorado Springs, CO 80918

Connecticut—36 Canterbury Lane, Mystic, CT 06355

Florida (all of the state except the southern tip)—433 N. Mills Ave., Orlando, FL 32803

Florida Gold Coast (southern Florida)—8571 S.W. 29th St., Miami, FL 33155

Georgia—1710 Walton Way, Augusta, GA 30904

Gulf (southeastern Texas)—3201 Wheeler, TSU Box 382, Houston, TX 77004

Hawaii—Department of Athletics, University of Hawaii, 1337 Lower Campus Rd., Honolulu, HI 96822

Indiana—155 W. Washington St., Suite 220, Indianapolis, IN 46204

Inland Empire (eastern Washington and northern Idaho)—S. 2016 Manito Pl., Spokane, WA 99203

Iowa—Box 1527, Welch Ave. Station, Ames, IA 50010

Kentucky—1515 Tyler Park Dr., Louisville, KY 40204

Lake Erie (northeast Ohio)—1607 Euclid Ave., Cleveland, OH 44115

Maine—10 Horton St., Lewiston, ME 04240

Metropolitan (New York and New Jersey around New York City)—Box 5340, FDR Station, New York, NY 10150

Michigan—Box 233, Flushing, MI 48433

Mid-Atlantic (eastern Pennsylvania, all of Delaware, and the southern tip of New Jersey)—Box 7321, Philadelphia, PA 19101

Midwestern (all of Nebraska and the western counties of Iowa)—Box 1522, Grand Island, NE 68801

Minnesota—4393 Arden View Ct., Arden Hills, MN 55112

Missouri Valley (all of Kansas and western Missouri)—620 W. 26th St., Kansas City, MO 64108

Montana—923 Avenue B, NW, Great Falls, MT 59404

New England (Massachusetts, Rhode Island, New Hampshire, and Vermont)—265 Medford St., Suite 102, Somerville, MA 02143

New Jersey (all but the southern part of the state)—Box 597, Red Bank, NJ 07701

New Mexico—141A Wyoming, NE, Albuquerque, NM 87123

Niagara (western New York)—Box 587, Buffalo, NY 14226

North Carolina—3125 Eton Dr., Raleigh, NC 27608

North Dakota—1310 Loy Ave., Wahpeton, ND 58075

Ohio (most of the state except the northeast corner) Box 44, Dayton, OH 45428

Oklahoma—5312 N. Vermont, Oklahoma City, OK 73112

Oregon (Oregon plus four counties in Washington)—Box 16120, Portland, OR 97216

Ozark (eastern Missouri and the southern tip of Illinois)—900 Weidman Rd., Manchester, MO 60311

Pacific (northern California and northern Nevada)—Box 1495, Fair Oaks, CA 95628

Pacific Northwest (northwestern Washington)—7212 E. Greenleaf Dr., N., Seattle, WA 98115

Potomac Valley (Washington, D.C., and parts of Maryland and Virginia)—5351 N. 37th St., Arlington, VA 22207

San Diego-Imperial (the two southernmost counties in California)—8148 Genesee Ave., #114, San Diego, CA 92122

Snake River (all of Idaho except the northern part plus northeast Nevada)—Box 4776, Pocatello, ID 83201

South Atlantic (most of Maryland)—1540 Chapel Rd., Havre de Grace, MD 21078

South Carolina—518 Lance Dr., Columbia, SC 29210

South Texas (the south-central part of the state)—523 Cave Lane, San Antonio, TX 78209

Southeastern (all of Tennessee and most of Alabama)—502 Alandale Rd., Knoxville, TN 37920

Southern (all of Louisiana and Mississippi)—12298 Sherbrook, Baton Rouge, LA 70815

Southern Nevada (the lower one-third of the state)—3013 King Midas Way, Las Vegas, NV 89102

Southern Pacific (southern California except around San Diego)—Box 4636, Downey, CA 90241

Southwestern (northeast Texas)—Box 22133, TWU Station, Denton, TX 76204

Three Rivers (western Pennsylvania)—1636 Princess Lane, Pittsburgh, PA 15236

Utah—855 California Ave., Salt Lake City, UT 84104

Virginia—3122 W. Clay St., #6, Richmond, VA 23230

West Texas (actually northwest Texas)—Box 2000, Lubbock, TX 79457

West Virginia—59 Canterbury Dr., Parkersburg, WV 26101

Wisconsin—1916 Campbell Rd., LaCrosse, WI 54601

Wyoming—819 W. 26th St., Cheyenne, WY 82001

Index